THE GALVANIZATION OF THE YOUNG VOTE IN THE 2008 PRESIDENTIAL ELECTION

Lessons Learned from the Phenomenon

Glenn L. Starks

University Press of America,® Inc.
Lanham · Boulder · New York · Toronto · Plymouth, UK

Copyright © 2010 by
University Press of America,® Inc.
4501 Forbes Boulevard
Suite 200
Lanham, Maryland 20706
UPA Acquisitions Department (301) 459-3366

Estover Road
Plymouth PL6 7PY
United Kingdom

Library of Congress Control Number: 2009933241
ISBN: 978-0-7618-4842-4 (clothbound : alk. paper)
ISBN: 978-0-7618-4843-1 (paperback : alk. paper)
eISBN: 978-0-7618-4844-8

This book is dedicated the family, friends and mentors who have supported me throughout my academic and professional careers. I wish to thank my mother, Mrs. Rosa D. Starks, niece, Ms. Erica S. Starks, and nephew, Mr. Kaleb Starks, for their support during the writing of this book. Their patience and dedication were unwavering. I also wish to thank a group of special friends and colleagues who were equally supportive: Mr. Teddy DuPree, Mr. F. Erik Brooks, Mrs. Bernadette L. Whitehead, Mrs. Charleen R. Trotter, and Mr. Miguel Zayas. I could never have gained the motivation to complete such an endeavor without the guidance of my professional mentors Mrs. Verona McLeod and Mrs. Brenda Longest, and my academic mentors at the L. Douglas Wilder School of Public Policy at Virginia Commonwealth University, Dr. Robert S. Holsworth and Dr. Blue Wooldridge.

A special thanks goes to Mr. Michael P. Austin of St. Louis, Michigan. Mr. Austin provided tremendous personal and professional assistance to the author in writing this book. His dedication and hard work were invaluable, as were his professional insights and academic assistance. This book is dedicated to his exemplary commitment to advancement of the field of public administration.

A special thanks also goes to the Center for Information and Research on Civic Learning and Engagement for permission to use data from its published research and fact sheets.

Contents

List of Tables

Introduction

The 2008 presidential election was the most historic election in United States history due to the diversity of the candidates and the outcomes of the election. An African American and female were the two leading contenders for the Democratic Party's presidential nomination. While African Americans overwhelmingly rallied behind Senator Barack Obama in the hopes of the nation electing its first African American President, many female voters enthusiastically supported the possibility of Senator Hillary Clinton becoming the nation's first female President. The Republican Party ran with a female as the Vice presidential candidate, Sarah Palin, further adding to the diversity of the election. Senator Obama won the Democratic nomination with the support of African Americans, Hispanics, young voters, and others who were attracted by his promise for sweeping changes in the government. He also benefited from the dissatisfaction voters had for former President Bush and Congress.

The election galvanized many segments of the U.S. population to exert their voting power, leading many who had never voted before to go to the polls. Voters rallied behind Senator Obama because of his ability to frame the problems the nation was facing. He was also able to lay out plans to correct these problems in a way that ordinary citizens could understand how his proposed changes would benefit them. His sermon-like speeches drew thousands of listeners to campaign rallies across the country. Beyond African Americans, he was particularly popular with young voters. Even before the general election, the enthusiasm of young Americans, their political involvement, and voter turnout percentages during primaries and caucuses reached historic levels.

With the election of Barack Obama as the first African American President of the United States, young voters who supported the Democratic Party feel the nation is finally moving to embrace diversity as they do, their concerns will being considered by government leaders, and their vote really does matter. Obama gained the majority of the popular vote because of support from young voters. Their sheer numbers and voter turnout rates during the 2008 election illustrate their political clout. This has created a unique situation in which the current level of political excitement and voting efficacy of young voters can be used in future presidential, state and local elections. This task will not be as easy as it sounds, however. Now that young voters feel the major political parties are listening to their concerns and taking their votes seriously, it will be incumbent upon those in office and parties to take actions that speak to the concerns and needs of young voters. They must also understand what caused young voters to be galvanized during the last election and capitalize on those lessons learned.

For young voters who supported the Republican Party, the same situation holds true. They also witnessed first-hand the importance of voting and their ability to influence the electoral process by getting involved. They too will expect the Republican Party to take greater actions to address their needs. If not, they may switch to the Democratic Party or cease staying involved in the political process.

Book Outline

The youth vote in the 2008 election challenged a theoretical belief that young Americans are apathetic, especially toward politics. It confirmed that just as with previous generations, young voters get involved when they feel matters that impact them are being espoused by political candidates. These members of Generation Y (term used to categorize those born after 1981 through 2000) can be energized if political candidates are able to appeal to their values and speak to their interests. While the interests of these groups may vary by individual, the interest of the entire group is theorized to be relatively homogenous.

This book explores the factors that led to the resurgence in youth voting during the 2008 presidential election, compare 2008 to youth voting historically, and discuss the future impact of the young voters on elections. It also explores the socio-economic characteristics of Generation Y and discusses their cultural interests and tendencies.

Chapter 1 explores the youth votes' impact on the 2008 presidential election, considering those voters 18 through 29 years old. Statistical data outlines the political support for the Democratic presidential ticket led by then Senator Barack Obama and the Republican ticket led by Senator John McCain. This chapter also explores the major issues that were of primary importance to young voters.

Chapter 2 provides a historical overview of youth voting in past elections, detailing what political parties and individual candidates they supported. It also discusses the issues that were of greatest concern for young voters and compares those to the most prominent issues during the 2008 election.

Chapter 3 discusses the population statistics and demographics of Generation Y, and outlines the factors that are theorized to influence their ideologies, motivations and interests. They are compared to other generations including the GI Generation (born 1901-1924), Silent Generation (born 1925-1942), and Baby Boomers (born 1943-1960), and Generation X (born between 1961 and 1980). Based upon generational theory, the differences in these generations lead them to be influenced by different factors.

Chapter 4 then explores methods to attract members of Generation Y to register and vote. These include interacting with potential young voters, using technology, and other strategies that have been used and can be used to get young voters to the polls. It also analyzes voting organizations and programs that target young voters, and the phenomenon of student activism.

Chapter 5 discusses the Democratic and Republican Party and the youth vote. This Chapter will explore the current platforms of each party. It will then discuss how these parties maintain members of all age groups and how they should work to maintain young voters.

Finally, Chapter 6 discusses the potential impact of youth voters on future elections.

Chapter 1: Youth Voting and the 2008 Presidential Election

The Need for Change: Theme of the 2008 Presidential Election

The 2008 election occurred when various crises were affecting the U.S. economy, domestic affairs, and foreign relations. The nation was in a recession due to rising gas prices, the falling value of the American dollar, and massive layoffs by companies across the country. The government was also taking actions deemed by some economists as "socialist" such as restrictive economic policies and a massive $700 billion bailout of private companies. Federal funds were poured into private financial institutions in an attempt to keep businesses from going bankrupt, insolvent or closing completely, and also to protect the investments of American citizens. The home mortgage crisis led to private companies, Fannie Mae, and Freddie Mac becoming almost insolvent and the largest percentage of foreclosed homes in U.S. history.

The U.S. government was still struggling to regain the trust of the American people after such incidents as the lack of government action after Hurricane Katrina. The government sat idle for days as thousands of American citizens died due to a lack of medicine, food, and shelter. When the government did finally react, the city of New Orleans was almost placed under a military and police state. The government debated the passing of laws that would significantly tighten immigration laws and prohibit gay marriage. Other major domestic issues included debates over reversing the Supreme Court decision in *Roe v. Wade* that had legalized abortion, passing stricter gun control laws, improving the nation's health care system to offer greater coverage to the uninsured, and reducing health care costs.

The United States was also fighting two wars overseas. The wars in Afghanistan and Iraq stemmed from the terrorists attacks of September 11, 2001, but arguments raged over the methods the administration used to begin and sustain the wars, and how and when the wars would ever end. These wars were straining U.S. relations with other countries as the costs to maintain forces overseas escalated, suspected terrorists were being held for years without trials in a detention camp in Guantanamo Bay (Cuba), the morality and legality of U.S. actions in interrogating prisoners was questioned, and the United States became more unpopular around the world due to the use of the Executive Branch's so-called "cowboy diplomacy" in taking international actions without consultation with U.S. allies. Tensions also existed with other countries including Cuba and Venezuela.

All of these issues were coupled with President George W. Bush loosing popularity and having the lowest approval rating of any U.S. President in history except Richard Nixon during Watergate. Bush's approval rating plummeted from a high of almost 90% immediately after September 11, 2001 to 22% by the time he left office in January 2009. Congress' rating was equally dismal. It fell from approximately 84% after September 11, 2001 to under 20% in 2008.

All of the aforementioned issues had a widespread and negative effect across the United States. Corporations, private businesses, educational institutions and ordinary citizens were all somehow impacted. Perhaps for the first time in history every politically active segment of the population felt they had a stake in the outcome of the 2008 election. For this reason, Senator Barack Obama's call for change and his accompanying slogan "Yes We Can" had widespread appeal to voters who desperately wanted the government to take some positive action to turn the country around. The Democratic Party pointed to failings of the outgoing Republican President and Republicans in Congress as the reason the country was suffering. They also cautioned voters that things would not change or even get worse if Republicans were allowed to run the Executive Branch or Congress for another term. Republican presidential candidate John McCain and his Vice presidential running mate, Sarah Palin, dubbed themselves as mavericks who would also bring change to the government through reforms and a radically different approach to governing than their Republican predecessors. However, they failed to convince the majority of the electorate they could bring about the change needed.

Obama's Appeal to Young Voters

The 2008 presidential election was perhaps the most historic in the U.S. after the election of George Washington as the first President. Barack Obama was elected as the first African American President to the dismay of many and fantasy of others. Most people interviewed on television and radio programs across the country gave almost the same response when asked their opinion about Obama being elected, "I never thought I would live to see this day". There were many other outcomes of the election that were also historically noteworthy, if not somewhat overshadowed. Obama was the first elected President born in the 1960s and born outside the continental United States, being born in Hawaii. Obama's running mate, Joe Biden, became the first Roman Catholic to be elected as Vice President. Biden is also the longest serving Senator in history to become Vice President. This was the first election with two U.S. Senators running against one another in a general election. Obama and McCain also made history due to their age differences. The difference of 25 years is the widest between two presidential competitors. Obama is the first Democratic candidate to be elected after losing the Ohio primary. His raw popular vote margin is the largest in history for a non-incumbent candidate. He received more popular votes than any presidential candidate in history. McCain, at 72 years of age, would have been the oldest person elected to President if he had won.

Obama entered the election as a relatively unknown Senator from Illinois. Because of his youth, political inexperience at the national level, lack of national visibility, and race he was not considered a serious contender for the Democratic nomination by many when he announced his intention to run for office, let alone a contender who could win the general election. He gained popularity through a grassroots campaign that inspired and mobilized supporters. His eloquent speaking ability and charisma were mesmerizing. His campaign rallies drew large audiences and his popularity was compared to "rock star" status. He quickly gained national media attention, elevating his national visibility. *Time* magazine voted Obama it's 2008 "Person of the Year" and explained the following in its special issue (Von Drehle, David 2008):

> The real story of Obama's year is the steady march of seemingly impossible accomplishments: beating the Clinton machine, organizing previously marginal voters, harnessing the new technologies of democratic engagement, shattering fundraising records, turning previously red states blue - and then waking up the day after his victory to reinvent the presidential-transition process in the face of a potentially dangerous vacuum of leadership. 'We always did our best up on the high wire', says his campaign manager, David Plouffe.

Obama gained popularity for three primary reasons: he was young, African American, and genuinely instilled hope in voters that he could change the failing policies of the federal government. Normally the first two reasons would be impediments for a candidate, as they have often been in the past. However, the social and cultural climate of the United States in the early 21st century presented a unique opportunity for a candidate with these characteristics. Even Obama's inexperience was attractive to voters. They believed he would bring a fresh perspective to Washington.

The beginning of the new century was a time when diverse groups were demanding racial and cultural changes and looking to the government to take an active role in bringing about these changes. Hispanics had staged protests across the nation in response to national, state and local laws that were attempting to strengthen anti-immigration laws. Hispanics felt these laws were unfair and discriminatory given their contribution to the nation's culture and economy. The gay and lesbian community was also protesting laws and court decisions that were banning same-sex marriages or reversing prior laws that allowed these marriages. In one of the most heated states, California voters approved a ballot proposition (Proposition 8) in November 2008 that amended the State Constitution to forbid any marriages that were not between a man and a woman. The controversy over this proposition had raged for months before the election, and California was one of several battlegrounds states that collectively led to a national debate on the issue. The African American community continued to struggle with issues of racial and social inequality. A protest was held in Jenna, Louisiana after six teenagers were given harsh legal punishments for beating up a fellow white student after an escalation of racial tension that was tolerated by the local school and local government. While 15,000 to 20,000 protestors gathered in Jenna to demand fair legal treatment for the African American students, similar marches and protests were held around the country. This issue led to resurgence in the national debate on race. The reversal of affirmative action programs by states and universities across the country, unarmed Black youths being killed by police officers in many urban cities, and the lack of proportional African American representation in top government positions contributed to this debate.

Inspired young voters began flexing their influence and political muscle due to Obama's appeal. Caroline Kennedy said that the primary reason she decided to support Obama was because she was convinced to do so by her children. In a speech she gave on January 28, 2008 she stated "They were the first people who made me realize that Barack Obama is the President we need". (Von Drehle, David, 2008)

The views of young voters were in line with the cultural, social and economic movements that were taking place across the nation. They were in support of racial, social and ethnic equality. Young Americans were equally tolerant of alternative lifestyles and accepting of homosexual couples. They were opposed to the wars and in support of improving the environment. At the same time, the policies, actions and decisions of President Bush and Congress on major issues were mostly in contradiction with the beliefs and values of the average young voter.

Obama was able to capitalize on all of these factors in his bid for President. His campaign gave young voters, and many other voting demographics, hope for the future and a feeling they had a candidate whose views reflected theirs and would take actions to address their concerns. He himself was young, culturally diverse (the offspring of a white mother and black father), and did not grow up rich. According to William Galston of the Brookings Institution speaking on Obama's appeal to young voters, "Part of it is generational identification. Many of today's young people have grown up in a multiracial, multiethnic context in part because of the enormous surge of immigration in recent decades. Senator Obama's internationalism is consistent with that. In addition, Senator Obama believes that people of good will with different views can get together around the table and solve problems. There are a lot of young Americans who would like to believe that's true." (Franceschi, 2008)

The news of Obama's election win on the night of November 4 led to spontaneous street parties in cities across the nation. Celebrations occurred in New York, Miami, Chicago, Washington D.C., Boston, Detroit, Seattle, Philadelphia, Denver, and Atlanta. These were not limited to the United States. Similar celebrations also took place in Toronto (Canada), Bonn and Berlin (Germany), Rio de Janeiro (Brazil), Sydney (Australia), and Kenya.

The Major Issues Surrounding the 2008 Presidential Election

The 2008 election signified the fourth major civic realignment in the United States. Civic realignment is defined as a major cultural, political and ideological change across the nation due to a major event. It occurs when the citizens of the nation demand and actively work for a change in national policy and federal governance. In other words, there is a major shift in national discourse impacting politics and governance. The first occurred in 1776 when the United States became an independent nation free from British rule. The second occurred in the 1860s when the nation fought a civil war predominantly because of slavery. The third occurred in 1932 as a result of the Great Depression. The 2008 election falls into this category because the nation faced an economic crisis, was engaged in foreign wars, and various segments of the population were demanding cultural and social equality. In all four cases, the outcomes of presidential elections were due to demands for change by the electorate.

Young voters were at the forefront of civic realignment in 2008. They were the most in favor of electing a candidate they believed would bring about political and social change. According to a survey of young voters, 50% of respondents believed McCain had the right experience to become President, compared to 34% who believed Obama did. However, a greater percentage of respondents believed Obama understood the problems of people their age (69%), could bring change (67%), and shared their values (52%). An article in *Time* magazine (Von Drehle, David 2008) summarized the concerns youth voters had during the election and why they thus supported Obama:

> Obama is tapping into a broad audience of energized young voters hungry for change, according to a new TIME poll of under-30 Americans. Nearly three-quarters of the respondents said they feel the country is headed down the wrong track, with majorities expressing worries about jobs, affordable health care and the war in Iraq. Their interest in the election exceeds their interest in celebrity news or sports - 7 of 10 said they are paying attention to the race. Obama is the only candidate in either party who is viewed favorably by a majority of young people, and he has half again as much support as his nearest competitor, Democrat or Republican.

The general feeling among all voters was that the nation needed change. According to a poll conducted by CBS and the New York Times in September 2008, 81% of all adults believed the United States was on the "Wrong Track". Of those surveyed by Rock the Vote!, 69% agreed. For young voters, this view significantly varied by political party. While 81% of young Democrats felt the nation was going in the wrong direction, 67% of Independent voters agreed compared to 49% of their Republican counterparts. By race, 67% of Whites and Latinos agreed, compared to 82% of African Americans.

Both Democrat and Republican young voters 18-29 years old were concerned about the economy. With less money to spend than older voters and many seeking to start their careers, it is not surprising this topped their list. The U.S. unemployment rate in 2008 was the highest in twenty-six years. The U.S. economy suffered the most serious downturn since the Great Depression.

Other primary concerns of young voters were the same as older voters, but were ranked differently. From the most to least important, young voters were concerned about rising gas prices, the wars in Iraq and Afghanistan, education and college costs, health care and prescription drug costs, and terrorism and Homeland Security. Other concerns for young voters were the federal budget deficit, immigration, government corruption and reform, taxes, the environment and global warming, moral values, social security and retirement, and gay rights.

Among all adults, the top concerns, starting with the most important, were jobs and the economy, terrorism and national security, gas prices, and health care.

The primary concerns of young voters also differed in order of importance by political party. For young Democrats, their top three concerns in descending order were jobs and the economy, Iraq, and health care and prescription drug costs. For young Republicans, the top issues were jobs and the economy, followed by terrorism and Homeland Security, and gas prices. Independents were also most concerned about jobs and the economy, followed by education and the cost of college, and Iraq. The next three paragraphs exemplify general the concerns of young voters on the issues of war, gas prices, and college costs.

Young voters, like their older counterparts, did not agree with how the government was running the war against terrorism. By the 2008 election, the trillion dollar war was being fought in two countries (Iraq and Afghanistan) and it was becoming more unclear as to how the government was planning to bring American troops home. According to some experts, opposition to the war may have been the primary factor that galvanized youth voting in 2004 and 2008. Per Harvard University election analyst Thomas Patterson (Franceschi, 2008),

> We forget now that in the summer of 2003 that Howard Dean rocketed upward in the polls and had a lot of youthful volunteers and his message was anti-Iraq. You go back to 1992, 1996 and 2000, the youth were barely there. Barely more than a third of them participated. In 2004 it was nearly 50 percent. That's a huge turnaround. And when you look at young people and what was on their minds, Iraq was the upper most issue... Since the start of this campaign in early 2007, I think what we've seen is a second source of energy for young voters and that's the Obama campaign. They were attracted to him in the first instance by his early opposition to the war in Iraq. At the same time, he happened to have the kind of personality, the kind of message that appealed to them.

The rising death toll of American troops and the stories of troops returning home traumatized led to youth opposition that was reminiscent of Vietnam. Obama capitalized on McCain's support of the war and McCain's statement that the U.S. could be involved for another 50 to 100 years when asked how much longer it would last.

Gas prices reached the highest levels in history in the years leading up to the 2008 election. In July 2008, the average national price for a gallon of unleaded gas was $4.11 and the price for a gallon of diesel was $4.84. While drivers significantly curbed their driving habits and struggled to afford gas just to go to work, gas companies continued to report the highest profits in history. For example, Exxon Mobil reported $11.68 billion in profits from total revenues of $138 billion for the second quarter of 2008 ($1,485.55 a second). As citizens looked to the government for action, the response from the Executive Branch was that the law of supply and demand would be allowed to control the market. Some critics charged that oil companies were deliberately cutting production to keep prices high. Congressional Democrats issued a press release in July 2008 stating "While oil companies are earning record profits and gas prices are soaring, the largest oil companies have invested more resources in stock buybacks than U.S. production". (Hargreaves, 2008)

College costs constantly increased during the decade leading up to the election. Including tuition, fees, room and board, the average 2008-09 academic year national cost for a private four-year school was $34,132, $14,333 for an in-state public four-year school, and $25,200 for an out-of-state four year school. The cost of a private school increased 4.8% from 2007, 5.7% for in-state public schools, and 5.2% for public four-year schools. (Musante, Kenneth 2008) Some students had to drop out of college because they couldn't afford it. Many of those who graduated were in debt for thousands of dollars due to student loans.

The aforementioned issues led to President Bush having the lowest public opinion rating than any other President in history except Richard Nixon. General disapproval was not because of the issues alone, but because many believed his administration either took direct actions that caused these problems or deliberately failed to take actions to stop them. Bush's disapproval was the greatest political handicap for the Republican Party. It was politically damaging for any Republican candidate to receive his endorsement or be seen with him at political functions. Historically, incumbent party leaders rally behind those running for office. In the 2008 election, there was a drastic attempt by Republican candidates to distance themselves from current party office holders, and especially President Bush. The Democrat Party even used past pictures of contenders with the President Bush in order to prove a Republican connection. McCain suffered with voters when he stated in an interview that he had supported Bush 90% of the time.

Obama's Connection to Young Voters and his use of Internet Campaigning

Obama used the internet as one of his primary sources of campaigning. The internet had been used effectively by candidates in prior elections and like many experts Obama recognized its viability in attracting voters, particularly young voters. According to Oshyn and Wang (2008), "A recent Harvard poll indicates that the candidates' entrees into technology to woo young voters may not be in vain - at the very least, their target audience is probably getting the message. According to virtually all of the respondents of the poll, who were between the ages of eighteen and twenty-four, the best way to contact them was via the Internet. E-mail was the number one means of access, with 84 percent saying that was the best way to reach them; Facebook came in second for those enrolled in four-year colleges (44 percent); and MySpace was second best for those not in a four-year college (34 percent)." In 2008, candidates took the use of the internet to new levels by going online to announce their intention to run for office, form committees, and hold meetings via online announcements. They set up MySpace and Facebook pages with personal information about themselves such as their favorite books, photographs, and event schedules.

During presidential campaigning, Obama's team established a website called VoteForChange.com that not only provided information about his campaign but also voter registration information. After taking office, President Obama established a new website called www.barackobama.com. This site posts messages and blogs from the President such as his weekly address, provides voter information, outlines extensive information on volunteering, allows users to donate to the Democratic National Convention (DNC), and allows users to join the site community. It also provides direct links to other internet sites the President can be found and that were used during his presidential campaign. These include Facebook, MySpace, YouTube, Flickr, Digg, Twitter, Eventful, Linkedin, BlackPlanet, Faithbase, Eons, Glee, MiGente, MyBatanga, AsianAve, and DNC Partybuilder.

Howard Dean was the first presidential candidate to demonstrate the effectiveness of internet campaigning. During his Democratic primary campaign in 2004, he used the web to raise money, organize volunteers, post speeches, host meetings, and distribute campaign information. He was particularly able to attract young voters online, who were called "Deaniacs" by supporters and "Deany Babies" by critics. Dean raised millions of dollars online, and gained so many supporters that he was eventually endorsed by major organizations and Democratic Party leaders. At one point, he was considered the frontrunner for the Democratic nomination. Although he lost the Democratic nomination, he made political history and set precedent with his internet campaigning.

Republicans also took lessons from Dean and applied them in the 2008 presidential campaign. Republican candidate Ron Paul broke all previous records with internet fundraising. In May 2007, he was the most popular online candidate of any Democratic or Republican candidate and dubbed an internet celebrity. Using YouTube, MySpace, Twitter, and Facebook, he garnered tremendous support and millions of dollars in donations. On December 16, 2007 he collected over $6 million in one day in internet campaign donations. His accomplishments were remarkable given the 72 year old candidate received money from individuals making small donations online rather than from large interest groups.

Obama used a three-fold tactic based on analyzing what had worked for Democratic and Republican candidates in the past. He used such traditional tactics as town hall meeting, rallies, and traveling the country to gain support. This solidified his support with voters of all ages. He utilized the internet to garner additional support and for fundraising. This proved invaluable in attracting young voters. Finally, he took a lesson from past candidates like Bill Clinton by actively and deliberately mobilizing young supporters. His campaign used young celebrities and political activists who became "youth directors" to go after young supporters. According to an article in *Time* (Von Drehle, 2008):

> Obama's outreach to students didn't spring from some starry-eyed principle. It started as a specific element of his early strategy in Iowa. The first-in-the-nation caucuses allow 17-year-olds to vote if they are going to turn 18 before the general election, which means most high

school seniors are eligible. To win those kids, Obama did something unusual in politics: he made them a genuine priority. After his rallies in towns across the state, he met backstage with student leaders from the area - a privilege most campaigns reserve for local VIPs and fund raisers. He also hired as his youth-vote coordinator Hans Riemer, a veteran of Rock the Vote!, which has been working to mobilize the student vote for years, with increasing success. Riemer extracted a promise that his work would be an integral part of the overall campaign, not a lip-serviced, photo-op'ed afterthought. His timing was perfect. The art of political organizing is in the midst of a broad philosophical overhaul that erases many of the old distinctions between young voters and their elders.

Unlike other candidates from both parties, Obama talked to and listened to young voters rather than talk down to them. He used the internet and young activists to go where young people could be found. In contrast, other candidates expected young voters to come to them. When they did, they were talked down to and often dismissed. Obama addressed their concerns and then instructed them on how to bring about change by not only relying on the government but by getting involved in government service. As will be discussed in Chapter 3, his message was effective with Generation Y because they are more engaged in community service projects and concerned about making a difference than previous generations.

By the end of the 2008 campaign, use of the internet and other technologies had been highly effective. According to the Pew Research Center (2008), "This year's presidential campaign witnessed unprecedented levels of online engagement in the political process as millions of ordinary citizens used the internet to keep informed about politics, donate money, share their views, join communities built around shared interests or objectives and mobilize others in support of their candidate. In the final days of the campaign, our colleagues at the Pew Research Center for the People and the Press found that 59% of voters had taken part in some sort of campaign activity online: 44% had sent or received campaign-related emails, 39% had watched online political videos and 37% had visited politically-oriented websites or blogs."

Voting Statistics from the 2008 Election Primaries and Caucuses

2008 saw an unprecedented interest by young voters in the presidential campaigns. Seventy-four percent of those polled by CNN said they were paying attending to the presidential campaigns, compared to 42% in the 2004 election and 13% in the 2000 election. The increase in youth voting was evident during the 2008 primaries and caucuses. They rallied to the polls in record numbers to support their favorite candidates. The greatest numbers voted in Democratic primaries because the party was offering extensive changes to the government and the possibility of the nation electing its first female or African American President. (Van Drehle, 2008)

Support from youth voters was overwhelmingly for Obama. Before the primaries, 29% of those polled said they would vote for Obama if a primary of caucus was held that day, compared to 20% for Clinton, 10% for Rudy Giuliani, 9% for McCain, 8% for Mike Huckabee, 6% for John Edwards, and 5% for Mitt Romney. Only 10% of voters were undecided.

Young voters significantly increased their participation during 2008 primaries and caucuses for both political parties from 2004 by a total of 103%. The following points summarize the states with the greatest percentage increases, as shown in **Table 1.1**:

- Iowa up by 133%: young Democrats from 17% to 22%
- Texas up by 301%: young Republicans from 9% to 13%
- Georgia up by 134%: young Democrats from 11% to 18%
- New York up by 160%: young Democrats from 8% to 15%
- Missouri up by 125%: young Republicans from 10% to 13%
- Oklahoma up by 188%: young Republicans from 9% to 14%

According to an article in *Time* (Von Drehle, David, 2008), "The excitement that created- a 'tidal wave', in the words of Bill Clinton - nearly drowned the hopes of the former President's wife. But Hillary Clinton answered with her own organizational prowess, whipping up huge numbers of working-class, female and older Democrats. Only the students have kept Obama in contention: in New Hampshire, his edge among young voters was 3 to 1; in Nevada, it was 2 to 1; and in Michigan, nearly 50,000 under-30s voted 'Uncommitted' because Clinton's name was the only one on the ballot."

More than 6.7 million young voters participated in the 2008 election primaries and caucuses, and 74% voted in Democratic primaries. As shown in **Table 1.2**, young voters comprised 14% of all Democratic primary participants, and 11% of participants in Republican primaries. Obama received 60% of the youth vote in Democratic primaries, compared to 38% for Clinton. In Republican primaries, the margin of support by candidate was not nearly as wide. McCain received 34% of youth votes, Huckabee 31%, Romney 25%, and 10% went to Paul. Primary voting was the leading indicator that youth voters would actually turn out on Election Day. Approximately 86% of those who voted during the primaries said they would likely vote on November 4, and 67% of those would be first-time voters.

As seen in **Table 1.3**, more than 3 million 18-29 year olds participated in Super Tuesday. The highest youth turnout rates were in Massachusetts (25%), Missouri (21%), and Georgia (21%). In comparison, the highest rates for voters 30 years old and over were in Massachusetts (40%), Illinois (37%), and Alabama (36%). Youth voters had the largest share of total voters in Utah (16%), California (14%), Massachusetts (14%), and Missouri (14%). Young voter turnout was higher in 2008 than in 2000 in every state (where data was available) except New York where it remained stable at 12%. For example, it was up by 13 points in Massachusetts and 14 points in Georgia.

Table 1.1: Youth (18-29 year olds) Voter Turnout at 2008 Primaries and Caucuses: 2008 increase over 2004

Source: Rock the Vote! (2008). "Young Voter Turnout 2008 – Primaries and Caucuses." (June 4, 2008), http://www.rockthevote.com/assets/publications/electronic-press-kit/young-voter-turnout-in-the.pdf

State	% increase	Dem increase	Rep increase
Total	103%	197%	18%
Iowa	133%	165%	53%
New Hampshire	50%	69%	29%
South Carolina	42%	182%	-22%
Florida	247%	268%	225%
Arizona	47%	118%	6%
California	58%	110%	-7%
Connecticut	167%	434%	28%
Delaware	222%	222%	
Georgia	126%	162%	83%
Massachusetts	139%	217%	43%
Missouri	125%	206%	61%
New York	160%	358%	-16%
Oklahoma	188%	107%	318%
Tennessee	209%	213%	203%
Louisiana	131%	240%	31%
Maryland	65%	183%	-27%
Virginia	95%	335%	-19%
Wisconsin	95%	95%	
Ohio	66%	218%	-27%
Rhode Island	806%	806%	
Texas	229%	435%	63%
Vermont	102%	102%	
Mississippi	402%	1032%	50%

Table 1.2: Summary of Youth Voters in State Primaries by Party: 2008

Source: Marcelo, Karlo Barrios and Kirby, Emily Hoban. *Quick Facts about U.S. Young Voters: The Presidential Election Year 2008*. Medford, Massachusetts: The Center for Information and Research on Civic Learning and Engagement, 2008.

Young Voters by Party

Democratic	Number of Primary Participants Share of Primary Participants	5,027,000 14%
Republican	Number of Primary Participants Share of Primary Participants	1,766,000 11%

Youth Voter Choice by Party

Democratic Choice	Republican Choice		
Clinton 38% Edwards 1% Obama 60%	McCain 34% Huckabee 31%	Paul 10% Romney 25%	

* There were no Republican exit polls for the following states so they were excluded from the Republican youth share: DE, IN, KY, MT, NM, NC, OR, PA, RI, SD, VT and WV.

Table 1.3: Super Tuesday Presidential Primary Participation in 2008: 18-29 Year Old Citizens Compared to All Voters

Source: Roscow, David. *Over Three Million Citizens Under the Age of Thirty Participate in Super Tuesday Primaries: Young Voters Support Obama and Huckabee and McCain.* Medford, Massachusetts: The Center for Information and Research on Civic Learning and Engagement, February 6, 2008.

Super Tuesday Primary State	Youth Turnout Rate in 2008	Youth Turnout Rate in 2000	Turnout Rate of Voters 30 and over	Overall Turnout Rate	Number of Youth Who Voted	Youth as Share of All Voters
Alabama	19%	N/A	36%	32%	135,597	13%
Arkansas	11%	N/A	29%	25%	48,112	9%
Arizona	7%	N/A	25%	21%	59,267	7%
California	17%	13%	32%	29%	873,508	14%
Connecticut	12%	7%	22%	20%	51,436	10%
Georgia	21%	7%	34%	31%	281,724	14%
Illinois	18%	N/A	37%	32%	377,996	13%
Massachusetts	25%	11%	40%	37%	231,022	14%
Missouri	21%	7%	35%	32%	190,863	14%
New Jersey	18%	N/A	32%	29%	187,889	11%
New York	12%	12%	20%	18%	311,833	13%
Oklahoma	14%	4%	33%	29%	82,609	13%
Tennessee	15%	3%	30%	27%	139,831	12%
Utah	15%	N/A	29%	25%	66,248	16%
Total					3,037,935	

Table 1.4 provides more detail on the number and percent of voters who participated in Super Tuesday primaries, while **Table 1.5** shows which candidate received the majority of youth votes. Over 2 million young voters participated in the Democratic primaries and approximately 938,000 in the Republican primaries. The largest Democratic primaries were held in California, New York, and Illinois. Democratic young voters had the largest share of total votes in Georgia (17%), Utah (17%) and California (16%). Obama won the youth vote in every state (a total of eleven) except for three that went to Clinton: Massachusetts, California and Arkansas.

The largest primaries for the Republican Party were held in California, Georgia, and Illinois. Young Republican voters had the largest share of total votes in Utah (16%), Oklahoma (14%), Massachusetts (13%), and Missouri (13%). McCain did not carry the largest number of states by youth voting, showing he did not even garner the majority of their support even just among Republican candidates. Rather, he gathered the largest number of votes because of his wins in California, Illinois and New York. The only other two states he won were Connecticut and New Jersey but these had smaller numbers of young voters. Huckabee won the most states for young Republican voters. He was the most popular in Alabama, Arkansas, Georgia, Missouri, Oklahoma, and Tennessee. McCain was also not the most popular Republican candidate among young voters in Arizona, his home state. Arizona was won by Romney, along with Massachusetts and overwhelmingly in Utah (88%) because he was a member of the Mormon Church.

Young voters helped the leading contenders of both parties win key primary states during Super Tuesday and subsequent primaries. Support from 25-29 year olds helped Clinton win the New Hampshire primary, and those 18-29 helped Obama win the Iowa caucus. Support from 18-29 year olds helped McCain win the California primary.

The highest youth voter turnout was among those who were college educated. While one in every four college-educated youths voted on Super Tuesday, only one in fourteen out-of-college youths voted. This trend carried over into the general election, as those without any college education comprised 24% of all voters 18-29. Those with no high school education only made up 4% of young voters. Sadly, these are perhaps the members of the U.S. population who have been most negatively impacted by the major issues surrounding the election. Per Rizga (2008), "There are close to 13 million 18- to 25-year-olds, who have never been enrolled in college in America. So far only about three million voted in the primaries. These non-college youths come disproportionately from lower-income backgrounds and African American and Latino communities. It is these very communities that stand to gain the most from more political power and resources, especially during the current recession." These groups are the most negatively impacted by a poor economy, lack of adequate health care, urban violence, a lack of government investment on the nation's infrastructure, and war because of their higher rates of military employment compared to college students.

Table 1.4: 2008 Super Tuesday Presidential Primary Participation by Political Party: 18-29 Year Old Citizens

Source: Roscow, David. *Over Three Million Citizens Under the Age of Thirty Participate in Super Tuesday Primaries: Young Voters Support Obama and Huckabee and McCain.* Medford, Massachusetts: The Center for Information and Research on Civic Learning and Engagement, February 6, 2008.

State	Democratic Primaries		Republican Primaries	
	Number of Primary Participants	Share of Primary Participants	Number of Primary Participants	Share of Primary Participants
Alabama	71,574	13%	64,023	12%
Arkansas	26,517	9%	21,595	10%
Arizona	31,201	8%	28,066	6%
California	645,965	16%	227,543	10%
Connecticut	34,929	10%	16,507	11%
Georgia	176,948	17%	104,775	11%
Illinois	290,660	15%	87,337	10%
Massachusetts	168,863	14%	62,159	13%
Missouri	114,863	14%	75,870	13%
New Jersey	143,497	13%	44,392	8%
New York	257,719	15%	54,114	9%
Oklahoma	36,149	9%	46,451	14%
Tennessee	79,663	13%	60,366	11%
Utah	20,847	17%	45,401	16%
Total	**2,099,395**		**938,599**	

Table 1.5: Super Tuesday Youth Vote Choice by Political Party

Source: Roscow, David. *Over Three Million Citizens Under the Age of Thirty Participate in Super Tuesday Primaries: Young Voters Support Obama and Huckabee and McCain.* Medford, Massachusetts: The Center for Information and Research on Civic Learning and Engagement, February 6, 2008.

State	Democratic Candidates			Republican Candidates			
	Clinton	Obama	Edwards	Huckabee	McCain	Paul	Romney
Alabama	32%	**64%**	2%	**51%**	22%	4%	24%
Arizona	37%	**59%**	5%	15%	32%	9%	**43%**
Arkansas	**56%**	43%	N/A	**68%**	16%	6%	7%
California	**51%**	47%	1%	23%	**34%**	7%	31%
Connecticut	39%	**58%**	2%	11%	**51%**	18%	9%
Georgia	23%	**75%**	2%	**43%**	23%	8%	24%
Illinois	29%	**69%**	2%	28%	**30%**	13%	22%
Massachusetts	**49%**	48%	N/A	4%	36%	6%	**52%**
Missouri	30%	**65%**	3%	**43%**	27%	9%	18%
New Jersey	39%	**59%**	N/A	8%	**46%**	17%	19%
New York	43%	**56%**	1%	15%	**43%**	11%	21%
Oklahoma	N/A	N/A	N/A	**38%**	26%	3%	28%
Tennessee	44%	**53%**	2%	**38%**	25%	14%	15%
Utah	25%	**70%**	N/A	2%	6%	4%	**88%**

Voting Statistics from the 2008 General Election

Obama decisively won the 2008 presidential election with 52.9% of the popular vote (66,882,230) and 365 electoral votes. McCain won 45.7% of the popular vote (58,343,671) and received 173 electoral votes. Eighty percent of Obama's 7.2% popular vote lead was due to the youth vote (6.8 million of the 8.5 million lead). The Democrats also won control of the Senate (58 seats versus 41) and the House of Representatives (257 seats versus 178). Fifty five percent of those polled who said race was a factor voted for Obama. Approximately the same percent who said race was not a factor also voted for Obama.

The 2008 election saw an increase of 8,875,857 voters of all ages over 2004, 66% of which was due to an increase in voters 18-19 years old (5,585,066). The turnout rate for voters 18-29 in 2008 was 53%, the highest since 18-20 year olds were given the right to vote in 1972 under the 26th Amendment. An estimated 23 million youth voted (see Chapter 2 for historical voting rates). The Democrats received the greatest support from young voters a percent of all voters in 2008 than in the last nine presidential elections. As shown in **Table 1.7** (based on exit polls), 66% of youth voters supported Obama compared to 52% of all voters. The only other prior election since 1972 near this 14% margin was in 2004 when 54% of youth voters supported Kerry compared to 48.1% of the total popular vote.

According to CNN exit polls, voters 18-29 year olds comprised 18% of all voters. The remaining age categories of voters were 30-44 (29%), 45-64 (37%) and 65 and older (16%). Obama garnered fewer percentages of votes as the age group of voters increased. Of those 18-29 years old, 66% voted for Obama and 32% for McCain (2% for other candidates). Within the group of voters 30-44, 52% voted for Obama compared to 46% for McCain. Approximately 50% of voters 45-64 voted for Obama and 49% for McCain, and 53% of those 65 and older voted for McCain and 45% for Obama. These statistics show a clear divide between young voters and older voters. These statistics hold true in most states. Even in McCain's home state of Arizona, 52% of voters 18-29 voted for Obama compared to 48% for McCain.

Table 1.6 provides statistics for the outcome of the election based on a CNN exit poll taken the night of the election. Obama received the largest percentage of votes from those who identified themselves as Democrats (89%) and Independents (52%), while McCain was overwhelmingly supported by Republicans (90%). Obama was also chosen by those who identified themselves as liberal (89%) and moderate (60%), while 78% of conservatives supported McCain. Obama was the primary choice by Blacks (95%), Hispanics (67%), Asians (62%) and those who identified themselves as "Other" (66%). The majority of White voters (55%) supported McCain. Interestingly, Whites comprised 74% of all voters. The combination of the 45% of White voters (particularly young White voters) and minority support led to Obama's victory. The majority of females (56%) also supported Obama, while 49% of males received his support.

Additional conclusions can be reached when analyzing education and income percentages. The more educated voters were, the more likely they were to support Obama. McCain received 68% of votes from those with no high school education (but they were only 4% of all voters), while Obama was supported by 51% of voters with some college (31% of all voters), 50% of college graduates (28% of all voters), and 58% of voters with postgraduate education (17% of all voters). McCain received the majority of votes from those with incomes over $100,000, which comprised 26% of all voters. Other notable groups that supported Obama were non-gun owners (65%) and those who did not support President Bush (67%). For example, Obama received Latino support because they had the greatest dissatisfaction with Bush's performance than any other group. According to CNN exit polls, 80% of Latinos gave Bush negative ratings compared to 72% of all Americans.

The 2008 Presidential Election and the Republican Candidates

The loss of the presidential election and many congressional seats were serious blows to the Republican Party. This was preceded by eight years of a Republican President whose approval rating had continually dropped, and growing dissatisfaction with the party by even some of its most loyal members. Many experts began to immediately question the party's ideology and the commonality it still had with the social, cultural, and religious beliefs and values of mainstream America. A day after the election, the party began reevaluating its platform, current and potential leaders, and what actions it needed to take to reestablish its political influence.

John McCain had lost his presidential bid for several reasons. First, he could not escape his ties to former President George W. Bush. Although McCain and his running mate ran with the motto that they were "Mavericks" who would bring sweeping reforms to Washington, the Democratic Party continuously and successfully reminded voters of McCain's voting record in supporting Bush's foreign and domestic policies. Second, McCain at times seemed to lack an understanding of how major issues were impacting average citizens. For example, he stated "the foundations of the economy are strong" when the nation was nearing a recession. Third, his running mate was a questionable choice given her inexperience with Washington politics. Sarah Palin had served as governor of Alaska for a short time (since 2006), and many wondered how McCain could question Obama's experience and then choose a running mate with even less. According to CNN (2008), "Sixty percent of those polled said the Alaska governor is not qualified to be president, if necessary; 38 percent said she is. That compares with the two-thirds of those polled who said Democratic vice presidential nominee Joe Biden is qualified to be president and the 31 percent who said he isn't."

Table 1.6: Demographic Voting Results of the 2008 Presidential Election

Source: CNN Exit Polls, Election Center 2008,
http://www.cnn.com/ELECTION/2008/results/polls/#USP00p1

	Size	Obama	McCain	Other / No Answer
Party				
Democrat	39%	89%	10%	1%
Republican	32%	9%	90%	1%
Independent	29%	52%	44%	4%
Ideology				
Liberal	22%	89%	10%	1%
Moderate	44%	60%	39%	1%
Conservative	34%	20%	78%	2%
Race				
Black	13%	95%	4%	1%
White	74%	43%	55%	2%
Hispanic	9%	67%	31%	2%
Asian	2%	62%	35%	3%
Other	3%	66%	31%	3%
Sex				
Female	53%	56%	43%	1%
Male	47%	49%	48%	0%
Religion				
Protestant	54%	45%	54%	1%
Catholic	27%	54%	45%	1%
Jewish	2%	78%	21%	1%
Other	6%	73%	23%	2%
None				
Family Income				
Less than $15,000	6%	73%	25%	2%
$15,000 - $29,999	12%	60%	37%	3%
$30,000 - $49,999	19%	55%	43%	2%
$50,000 - $74,999	21%	48%	49%	3%
$75,000 - $99,999	15%	51%	48%	1%
$100,000 - $149,999	14%	48%	51%	1%
$150,000 -	6%	48%	50%	2%

$199,999				
Over $200,000	6%	52%	46%	2%
Education				
No High School	4%	63%	35%	2%
High School Grad	20%	52%	46%	2%
Some College	31%	51%	47%	2%
College Graduate	28%	50%	48%	2%
Postgraduate study	17%	58%	40%	2%
Union Membership				
Union Member	12%	59%	39%	3%
Non-Union Member	88%	51%	47%	2%
Age				
18 – 29	18%	66%	32%	2%
30 – 44	29%	52%	46%	2%
45 – 64	37%	50%	49%	1%
65 and older	16%	45%	53%	2%
Age and Race – White				
18 – 29	11%	54%	44%	2%
30 – 44	20%	41%	57%	2%
45 – 64	30%	42%	56%	2%
65 and older	13%	40%	58%	2%
Sexual Orientation				
Heterosexual	96%	53%	45%	2%
Gay, Lesbian or Bisexual	4%	70%	27%	3%
Gun Ownership				
Gun in Household	42%	37%	62%	1%
No Gun	58%	65%	33%	2%
Bush Approval				
Approve of Bush	21%	10%	89%	1%
Disapprove of Bush	71%	67%	31%	2%

Table 1.7: Democratic Presidential Share of the Youth Vote (18-29 year olds) Compared to Share of the Total Popular Vote

Source: Blades, Meteor. "Youth Voter Turnout Up, But Fails to Break '72 Record." *Daily Kos* (November 5, 2008), http://www.dailykos.com/storyonly/2008/11/5/171841/524/28/654938

Election Year	Share of the Youth Vote	Share of the Popular Vote
1972	48%	37.5%
1976	51%	50%
1980	44%	41%
1984	40%	40.4%
1988	47%	45.5%
1992	43%	42.9%
1996	53%	49.2%
2000	48%	48.3%
2004	54%	48.1%
2008	66%	52%

One of the reasons Palin was chosen was to attract the female vote that Hillary Clinton had garnered, and counter the Democrat's possibility of the first African American President with the Republican Party offering the possibility of the first female Vice President. But Palin angered some women with her disapproval of abortion. She was also politically harmed by constant negative media attention. She was ridiculed almost weekly on such comedy programs as Saturday Night Live and Comedy Central's the Daily Show due to her accent, odd use of adjectives, and distortions of facts. Some of the most ridiculed comments she made during the campaign were an interview statement she made inferring she could see Russia from her house (in Alaska), her nicknaming of middle and lower class Americans as "Joe Six-Pack" to mean "average Joes", and her constant referencing of herself as just an "Average Hockey Mom".

McCain and Palin did have some areas of popularity. McCain's war record and years spent as a prisoner of war garnered support from the military, veterans and many other patriotic groups. He had years of experience in Washington, having served in Congress since 1983. He had voted against his party in the past on key issues, showing he would not compromise on some issues simply because of party affiliation. These issues included President Bush's tax cuts, gun legislation, and his support of Republican Senator Jim Jeffords when Jeffords decided to become an Independent. Palin garnered support from raising a special needs child and her ability to therefore relate to families in similar situations. She also exemplified a working mother who had to balance the demands of a career and raising a family.

In the end, McCain was unable to attract a majority of young voters because they couldn't relate to his message. According to William Galston, "McCain speaks an older political language. It's the language of duty and obligation and responsibility, rather than choice and liberty. He is calling the citizens of the United States to a kind of citizenship that they haven't been urged to embrace for decades. And it remains to be seen just how potent that appeal will be." (Franceschi, 2008)

Chapter 2: Youth Voting During Past Presidential Elections

Historical Youth Voter Turnout Rates

Voter turnout rates in the United States have been on a steady decline since the 1960s (see **Table 2.1**), even though the voting age population has constantly increased. In 1960, 63.1% of the voting age population cast ballots in the presidential election. Over 65% of eligible voters registered, and over 90% of those registered voted. The highest turnout rates since the 1960s were in 1972 (55.2%), 1992 (55.1%) and 2004 (55.3%). In each of these election years, the presidential races were heated contests between a Democratic challenger campaigning for change and an incumbent Republican administration.

American youth were politically and socially active in the 1960s and early 1970s due to their interest in civil rights and more so by the Vietnam War. After 18-20 year olds were given the right to vote in 1972, young people generally became apathetic about voting due to their perception of the government's ignoring their interests. Their sentiments echoed that of the general population. The government was seen by many as ineffective, not concerned about serving the needs of average citizens, and more concerned about catering to the rich and powerful interest groups. For example, Republican Presidents have often espoused the principle of "trickle-down economics" and similar practices that produce benefits for the wealthiest Americans and big businesses with the goal of financial benefits flowing down to the middle and lower class.

The fall in voter turnout was a surprise given that experts in the 1950s and 1960s believed trends were occurring that would increase voter participation. As more Americans became educated, experts believed this would lead to an upswing in voter participation. Education is perhaps the leading socio-economic factor with a positive correlation to voting. Women were voting in increasing numbers and fast approaching the rates of men. However, some women found it hard to support an institution being led predominantly by men, and many top leaders did not support issues important to most women such as abortion rights and equal pay. The passing of the Civil Rights Act of 1964 removed voting barriers for African Americans by making it illegal for literacy tests, polls taxes and other illegal conditions to vote. However, there were few candidates who showed genuine interest in advancing such causes as affirmative action in education, ensuring civil rights laws were being enforced, and removing barriers prohibiting African Americans from rising in positions of prominence in government and business.

The 26th Amendment was adopted on July 1, 1971, reducing the legal and standardized U.S. voting age to 18 from 21. The amendment was introduced because 18 year olds could be drafted and die for their country but were not allowed to vote. The nation was in the midst of the Vietnam War and student protests were taking place around the country in opposition to the war. These protests added additional pressure on Congress and the Executive Branch to reduce the voting age. The amendment was endorsed by Presidents Dwight D. Eisenhower, Lyndon B. Johnson and Richard Nixon.

The initial law to reduce the voting age from 21 to 18 was passed under the Voting Rights Act of 1970. Oregon and Texas challenged the law on the grounds that it not only mandated a new voting age at the national level but for state and local levels as well. The Supreme Court ruled in *Oregon v. Mitchell*, 400 U.S. 112 (1970) that the mandate beyond the national level was unconstitutional, violating the sovereign powers of the states. This created impending confusion for the 1972 election, with all voters being able to vote for federal candidates but only voters 21 and over being able to vote for state and local candidates unless they lived in a state that had laws that had reduced the voting age to 18. The ratification of the 26th Amendment overturned the Supreme Court's decision.

During the 1972 general election, Republican Presidential incumbent Richard Nixon defeated Democratic opponent Senator George McGovern (South Dakota) by a margin of 23.2% in the popular vote, the fourth largest margin in presidential election history. Nixon received 520 electoral votes versus 17 for McGovern. Over 69% of the 140,776,000 in the voting age population registered to vote, and 63% of the voting age population actually voted (87.1% of those that registered).

The participation of young voters in general elections declined steadily after 1972. During the 1972 election, the turnout rate for 18-29 year olds was 55% of those eligible to vote. It fell to under 50% for each subsequent election (1976, 1980, 1984 and 1988), until the 1992 election when it again exceeded 50%. During the 1996 and 2000 elections, the percentage fell to approximately 40% for each year. Young voters again felt disenfranchised and disconnected with politicians and political parties. Candidates running for office did not address issues young voters were concerned about. Most dismissed the importance of young voters in winning elections.

In 2004, the turnout for young voters increased to 49% and it increased again during the 2006 mid-term elections (i.e. congressional elections). Several factors led to this increase. First, candidates became more concerned about the same issues as young people. As young people became more educated, they were concerned about more serious issues such as the economy and the environment. Second, younger generations comprise a larger percentage of the voting age population and thus their political influence grew. Third, candidates were younger and more culturally diverse, reflecting the demographics of young America. At the national, state and local levels African-American, Hispanic, female, homosexual and other minority candidates were running for offices and seeking support from within their own demographic groups and young voters who were more accepting of people from different races, ethnicities and backgrounds. Finally, increases in organized programs to get young people registered to vote, technological advancements that made information more accessible, and the influence of popular culture led to greater involvement.

Table 2.1: Voter Turnout in General Elections: 1960 - 2004

Source: Federal Election Commission,
http://www.infoplease.com/ipa/A0781453.html

Year	Voting-age population	Voter registration	Voter turnout	Turnout of voting-age population (percent)
2004	221,256,931	174,800,000	122,294,978	55.3
2000	205,815,000	156,421,311	105,586,274	51.3
1996	196,511,000	146,211,960	96,456,345	49.1
1992	189,529,000	133,821,178	104,405,155	55.1
1988	182,778,000	126,379,628	91,594,693	50.1
1984	174,466,000	124,150,614	92,652,680	53.1
1980	164,597,000	113,043,734	86,515,221	52.6
1976	152,309,190	105,037,986	81,555,789	53.6
1972	140,776,000	97,328,541	77,718,554	55.2
1968	120,328,186	81,658,180	73,211,875	60.8
1964	114,090,000	73,715,818	70,644,592	61.9
1960	109,159,000	64,833,096[*]	68,838,204	63.1

*Registrations from AL, AK, DC, IA, KS KY, MS, MO, NE, NM, NC, ND, OK, SD,
WI, and WY not included

Table 2.2 shows the voter turnout rates for those 18-21, 18-29, and voters 30 and over for each presidential election from 1972 through 2008. In 1972, 18-21 year olds had a turnout rate of 48% in this first election they were eligible to vote. The turnout rate for those 18-29 was 55% and those 30 and over had the highest rate at 70%. The rates for those under 30 declined for the next four elections until twenty years later. In 1992, 51% of those 18-29 voted and the rate for 18-21 years old was 40%. The rates for those 30 and over remained high from 1972 through 1992, with only minor decreases in 1976 and 1988.

All groups showed a decline in the 1996 and 2000 elections. The youth turnout rate increased in the 2004 general election and the 2006 congressional election. These were the highest turnout rates and the first three-year trend of increases since 1972. In 2004, the turnout rate for those 18-29 increased by 9% from 2000 to 49%, and the rate for 18-21 year olds increased by 12% to 42%. The rate for young voters increased at rates that far outpaced those 30 and over. The rate for the later group only increased by 3%.

Table 2.3 provides voter turnout rates by age, race and ethnicity for the 1972 through 2004 presidential elections. African American youths have had the highest rate increases of any other group. In 1972, their turnout rate was 37.5%. By 2004, their rate had reached 47.3%. This rate was almost as high as Whites in the same age group (49.8%). The rates in 2004 also increased for Latinos, Asians and Native Americans. After 1972, the rates for White youths were highest in 1992 when Bill Clinton, George H.W. Bush and Ross Perot ran for office. This year saw the second highest rates for African Americans and the second highest rates for Latinos and Native Americans. Comparable trends were found for those 18-24 and 18-29. These rates show that young voters get engaged when candidates make an active effort to attract young voters (as Bill Clinton did) and when young voters are attracted to candidates because they can relate to issues surrounding the election.

Experts agree that candidate attention to young voters has been the key factor leading to increased turnout. Per a report from the Graduate School of Political Management at The George Washington University (2006), "Leading campaign professionals, analysts and academics agree that one of the key factors driving this recent increase in turnout is that there has been, for the first time in decades, a major investment in mobilizing these voters. Non-partisan organizations that ran peer-to-peer field operations, media, and visibility campaigns spent an estimated $40 million on registering and turning out young voters, a presidential campaign made a media buy targeting young voters, and partisan organizations both inside and outside of the party structures mobilized supportive youth."

Table 2.2: Voter Turnout in Presidential Election Years by Age Group: 1972 - 2008

Source: Kirby, Emily Hoban and Kawashima-Ginsberg, Kei. "The Youth Vote in 2008." Medford, Massachusetts: The Center for Information and Research on Civic Learning and Engagement, April 2009, http://www.civicyouth.org/PopUps/FactSheets/FS_youth_Voting_2008.pdf

| | Age Group, Turnout Rate | | |
	18-21	18-29	30 and older
1972	48%	55%	70%
1976	39%	49%	68%
1980	36%	49%	71%
1984	37%	49%	71%
1988	34%	44%	69%
1992	40%	51%	72%
1996	31%	40%	64%
2000	30%	40%	65%
2004	42%	49%	68%
2008	48.5	51%	67%

Table 2.3: General Election Voter Turnout by Age Groups, Race and Ethnicity for 18-24 year olds: 1972-2004

Source: Lopez, Mark Hugo, Emily Kirby, and Jared Sagoff. *The Youth Vote 2004*. Medford, Massachusetts: The Center for Information and Research on Civic Learning and Engagement, July 2005. (using data compiled from the CPS November Youth and Registration Supplements, 1972 – 2004)

| | Age Groups | | | | 18-24 by Race and Ethnicity | | | | |
	18-24	25 and older	18-29	30 and over	White, Non-Hispanic	African American, Non-Hispanic	Latino	Asian, Non-Hispanic	Native American, Non-Hispanic
1972	52.1%	68.4%	55.4%	69.5%	54.2%	37.5%	*	*	*
1976	44.4%	65.4%	48.8%	67.0%	47.5%	29.8%	28.6%	*	*
1980	43.4%	68.5%	48.2%	70.6%	46.4%	32.4%	25.6%	*	*
1984	44.3%	68.9%	49.1%	71.2%	45.5%	44.1%	32.6%	*	*
1988	39.9%	65.8%	43.8%	68.5%	41.3%	37.8%	28.3%	*	*
1992	48.6%	70.5%	52.0%	72.4%	52.0%	40.6%	33.1%	31.7%	36.5%
1996	35.6%	61.6%	39.6%	63.6%	37.7%	33.8%	24.0%	35.0%	25.0%
2000	36.1%	62.9%	40.3%	64.6%	38.1%	36.2%	25.6%	27.8%	30.1%
2004	46.7%	66.3%	49.0%	67.7%	49.8%	47.3%	33.0%	35.5%	36.6%

* Were classified as "other" during these years

The resurgence of youth voting has led to other positive impacts on youth and society. Per Karlos Barrios Marcelo of the Center for Information and Research on Civic Learning and Engagement (CIRCLE) in a speech at the Foreign Press Center Briefing (2008),

> This generally means they're probably involved in other activities such as following the news more carefully; maybe having closer ties with certain social groups. This is good in general because young people, what we find in the research, when they're tied to these kind of social organizations and public institutions, they have lower rates of high school dropout; there's lower violence and teen crime; there's lower pregnancy rates; so all around it's good for young people to be involved in the sort of civic part of society. And having an increasing voter turn rate is a good sign that some of that is going on right now.

The next three sections summarize the campaigns and results of the 1960, 1992, and 2004 presidential elections. These discussions outline how candidates have either been successful in attracting young voters or turning them away. Analyzing these elections creates an equation that explains higher youth voter turnout during recent elections:

Increased youth voter turnout = Minority voters + higher education + higher income + interest in candidates

Interest in candidate = Youth interest in campaign issues + youth compatibility with candidate ideology

1960 Presidential Election (Kennedy v. Nixon)

John F. Kennedy is considered the first modern presidential candidate to galvanize young people to vote and join public service. His young age, charismatic nature, and progressive stance on governance attracted young voters. During his presidential inauguration address, Kennedy spoke words that epitomized call to young Americans: "Let the word go forth from this time and place, to friend and foe alike, that the torch has been passed to a new generation of Americans." The national voter turnout rate for the 1960 election was 63.1%, and no election since has seen a rate that high. Barack Obama has been compared to President Kennedy, and the similarities between the two can be found when analyzing the circumstances of the 1960 election.

The 1960 election was one of the closest presidential races in history and was an election of firsts. Kennedy was the youngest candidate ever elected President. He also became the first Roman Catholic elected President. His competitor, Richard Nixon, was the former Vice President and had turned that position into a major political office. He was the first Vice President to run for President with that distinction. It was the first election in which the ban on a sitting President running for a third time was in effect. The 22nd Amendment was passed in 1951. If it had not been passed, President Dwight D. Eisenhower (who had already served two terms in office) might have easily won the election due to his popularity. However, it is doubtful that he would have run due to health issues and his desire to retire. Kennedy and Nixon were the first presidential contenders who were both born in the 20th century. It was the first election in which Alaskans and Hawaiians were allowed to vote for President since they had both been granted statehood in the previous year. It was also the first presidential election with televised debates.

Kennedy had to overcome several social prejudices. His opponents campaigned that Kennedy was too young and inexperienced to be President. They suggested that he should run as the running mate of a more experienced candidate. In response to this, Kennedy publicly stated "I'm not running for Vice President, I am running for President." His religion was also controversial. Many did not believe non-Catholic voters would support Kennedy and others believed his religion would cause him to make biased decisions. Some believed he would take instructions from the Pope. During a campaign speech, he promised he would obey the Constitutional principle of separation of church and state. His win during the West Virginia primary, thought to be one of the primary states where anti-Catholic bigotry was widespread, squelched beliefs that voters would not support his candidacy. Kennedy was very popular among African Americans. He gained their support by calling local political leaders and authorities in Georgia when civil rights' leader Martin Luther King, Jr. was arrested, and also spoke to King's father and wife. Nixon, on the other hand, refused to get involved.

Kennedy's campaign was masterfully run by his brother, Robert Kennedy, and he defeated all other Democratic contenders. He even defeated then powerful Senate Majority Leader Lyndon B. Johnson, and Adlai Stevenson, the party's nominee in the 1952 and 1956 elections. Kennedy shocked many when he then asked Johnson to be his running mate. Many of Kennedy's staff, liberal Democrats, and even Robert Kennedy opposed the choice of Johnson, but Kennedy felt he needed Johnson to win southern states.

Nixon faced little opposition for the Republican nomination. His only serious competitor was Governor Nelson Rockefeller from New York who later withdrew due to Nixon's perceived popularity. Nixon was most harmed in his general election race by two events. When President Eisenhower was asked to give an example of a time when he had been given valuable advice by Nixon, Eisenhower replied "If you give me a week, I might think of one." Although it was later revealed he was joking, this remark caused Nixon to lose popularity. The most damaging event was the first of four televised presidential debates. Nixon looked pale, tired and agitated. Kennedy, on the other hand, was tan, relaxed and knowledgeable. These debates damaged voter's perception of Nixon, but drew viewers closer to Kennedy.

Kennedy won the election by the closest popular-margin vote in the 20th century. He received 34,220,984 votes (49.7%) compared to Nixon's 34,108,157 (49.5%). The race was so close that Nixon did not concede to Kennedy until November 9. Kennedy won 303 electoral votes compared to 219 for Nixon.

Nixon was the first presidential candidate to lose the election but still win more than half of the states (26 states).

1992 Presidential Election (Clinton v. Bush)

The 1992 presidential election was between incumbent George H. W. Bush (Republican), Democratic candidate William Jefferson "Bill" Clinton (Governor of Arkansas), and Independent Ross Perot (Texas businessman). The nation was struggling to recover from a recession, the national debt was escalating, and many Americans were pessimistic about the future direction of the country. Although President Bush believed he could win reelection based on the nation's victory in the Gulf War and the still high popularity of former President Ronald Reagan, his chances were seriously hindered by the other problems created under this presidency.

Just as Kennedy had done in 1960, Clinton was able to attract young voters with his charismatic appeal, ability to outline clear goals, and even because of his somewhat radical past. He actively sought young voters by campaigning on college campuses across the country. He appeared on MTV and such programs as the Arsenio Hall Show, candidly answered very poignant questions even when they were about his personal life. Republican candidates, on the other hand, declined invitations from these types of media.

During the campaign, Bill Clinton, Hillary Clinton, vice presidential candidate Al Gore and his wife Tipper all held rallies on college campuses around the country to unite young voters to support the Democratic ticket. They spoke to issues of interest to young people such as the environment. The Republicans perhaps assumed young people would vote Republican because of Ronald Reagan's popularity when he was in office. Young voters had voted predominantly Republican in the 1988 election when George H.W. Bush defeated Michael Dukakis.

Clinton won the election with 44,909,326 votes (43%), compared to 39,103,882 for Bush (37.4%), and 19,741,657 for Perot (18.9%). Forty-three percent of voters 18-29 supported Clinton, compared to 34% for Bush and 22% for Perot. Clinton received 370 electoral votes, Bush 168, and Perot received none. Bush not only lost the general election because of Clinton's popularity with Democrats, but he also lost support from within the Republican Party by breaking his 1998 campaign pledge to not raise taxes. His words in that campaign, "Read my lips, no new taxes", are one of the most memorable statements made by a presidential candidate.

Clinton's popularity with young voters grew during his first term in office. When he ran for reelection in 1996, he received 53% of youth votes compared to 34% going to Bob Dole and 10% to Perot.

2004 Presidential Election (Bush v. Kerry)

There were 41.1 million 18-29 year olds eligible to vote in 2004, and 30 million actually voted (49%). The turnout rate for young voters was more than double any other age group. More notable than the increased turnout rate was the fact that 81.6% of young people that registered actually voted. This demonstrates that the biggest opportunity to increase youth voting is by getting them to register. The majority of young voters were White (67.5%), 15.3% were Black, 13.2% Hispanic, 2% Asian, and 2% identified themselves as "Other". Females (53.7%) had higher rates than Males (46.3%). T

The increase in youth voting in the 2004 election was partly due to African American youths. Their turnout rate increased by over 11% from the 2000 election for those 18-24 year old to 47.3%. The turnout rates for Blacks was just 2.5 percentage points below White youth and was the highest turnout rate of any racial or ethnic minority group.

By education level, those with college degrees continued to have higher turnout rates than those will some or no college education. College students learn about the importance of political engagement and civic duty in college, and also get engaged in social and fraternal groups that often have programs geared toward community improvement.

Although Democratic candidate John Kerry lost the election to George W. Bush, Kerry received 54% of the vote from 18-29 year olds. His greatest support came from minority youths. Eighty-eight percent of African Americans and 58% of Hispanics supported Kerry, compared to 44% of White non-Hispanic youths. Bush won the election by gaining votes from White non-Hispanic voters who were 30 and over. Fifty-nine percent of them supported Bush, compared to 11% of African Americans and 45% of Hispanics.

The election saw a break from political ideology among young voters that resulted in a shift in candidate support. This shift was one of the impetuses for the Democrats winning the presidency and the majority of congressional elections in 2008. It began with young voters being dissatisfied with the direction national leaders were taking the country. In 2000, 59% of young voters believed they were "better off today than four years ago." By 2004, only 35.2% felt this way. In 2000, 36.1% of young voters identified themselves as being Democrat, and 36.9% did in 2004. In comparison, 24.7% identified themselves as Republican in 2000 and 34.5% were in 2004. However, some of those that identified themselves as Republican voted Democrat. While 47.6% of youth voted Democrat in 2000, 53.6% voted Democrat in 2004. This is compared to 46.2% voting Republican in 2000 and 45% in 2004. (Marcelo, et.al. 2008) This move to the left in voting by Republican voters is indicative of what happens when there is a recession or other condition in which voters believe the government should take a more active role.

Obama's Similarity with Past Presidents

Obama's youthful enthusiasm and eloquent speeches appealed to voters in the same manner that they were drawn to former Presidents John F. Kennedy and Bill Clinton. All three men were young presidential candidates that were active, progressive, and could deliver messages that appealed to many segments of the population, particularly younger voters. Their charismatic natures added to their appeal.

Kennedy, Clinton and Obama each ran for office during times when the United States was facing major issues that had the potential of changing the country politically, economically and culturally. Kennedy ran in 1960 when the primary foreign affairs concerns were the Cold War with the Soviet Union and the nation was being transformed due to the civil rights movement. His campaign focused on bringing about change and ushering in a "New Frontier". Kennedy succeeded in attracting young voters to the Democratic Party and instilling enthusiasm for getting involved in politics and obtaining jobs in government service. Many of those he influenced that were still alive in 2008 were still members of the Democratic Party.

Besides both being young Democratic leaders, Obama and Kennedy were both presidential candidates who successfully overcame issues of historical bias. While Obama overcame his race being a political impediment, Kennedy overcame concerns about him being. Kennedy is still the only Catholic to ever have held the office of President. They each also faced charges by their opponents that they were politically inexperienced compared to their opponents. Kennedy was 43 when he began running for office and had served thirteen years in the U.S. Congress from Massachusetts as a member of the House of Representatives and then as Senator. His opponent, Richard Nixon, had served in both houses of Congress for seven years and was Vice President under Eisenhower from 1953 until 1961. Obama was 47 when elected and had only served three years in Congress as a Senator from Illinois. McCain served in the House of Representatives from 1983 to 1987 and in the Senate since 1987. Both Kennedy and Obama used their charisma, personal appeal, knowledge, political skills, and the ability to inspire voters to win the presidency.

Bill Clinton was also one of this nation's youngest Presidents. He was 46 when sworn into office. He served as Governor of Arkansas from 1978 through 1980 and again from 1982 through 1992. When he ran for president against incumbent George H.W. Bush, the United States was in a recession. Clinton captured 43% of votes for those 18-29 in 1992 and 53% of their vote when he ran for reelection in 1996. Clinton was charismatic, calm under pressure, and had an impressive grasp on difficult issues such as the U.S. economy. Kennedy and Obama were also calm under pressure, and all three remained so during televised debates while their presidential opponents appeared agitated.

Chapter 3: Generational Theory and Generation Y

Generational Theory

Generational theory holds that different generations can be defined by the range of years they were born. American history can be viewed through the framework of a repeating cycle of general attitudes within a population. People who are born and raised within the same cycle (consisting of approximately 20 years) share common experiences from youth through elderhood and thus possess common psychological, motivational, and cultural attitudes and beliefs. These years are segregated based upon distinct social, economic, and political factors that occurred over a period of time resulting in the members of a particular generation having shared experiences that impact them in the same or similar ways. For example, those born between1925 and 1942 were all somehow impacted by the Great Depression, World War II, and the revolutions in military, academics and industry.

Members of the same generation are considered "cohorts". Strauss and Howe (1991) used the term to define those within the same generation. Cohorts begin to develop shared perceptions in childhood. Hagevik (1999) believed, "The beliefs you accumulated as a kid effect how you now view risk and challenge, authority, technology, relationships, and economics, as well as whom you hire, fire, or promote. Your 'cohort beliefs' continue to make a difference, although it should be noted here that the cohorts are not absolute categories but descriptive devices."

Generational theory does not postulate that every member of a generation is impacted by events the same way, or that they will think and act the same way. Their desires and attitudes may differ. Esklilson and Wiley (1999) surveyed undergraduate students in sociology courses at four institutions to determine if they exhibited parallel aspirations for the future, such as similar desires to have a family and gain financial success. While they found the homogeneity expected of a generational cohort, the desires of the group were affected by the race, gender and social class (due to income and education). Additionally, their principal concerns were not foreign to the values their elders might have expressed when they were the same ages. Still, members of the same cohort will share many general values, perceptions and attitudes due to their common experiences and influences.

Table 3.1 outlines the characteristics of generations born in the United States during the 20th century. Each of these five generations can be defined based upon the years its members were born and the primary factors that impacted their upbringing: the predominant family structure children were raised in, the jobs and employment experiences of their parents, the level of society's technological advancement, the and primary events that influenced their thinking, behaviors, and daily lives.

The G.I. Generation (1901-1924) was born into stable two-parent homes when the United States was booming industrially. As adults, they won World

War II, thus gaining their name and similar titles such as the Great Generation and the G.I. Joe Generation. The Silent Generation (1925-1942) was named so not only because they are the smallest generation of the 20th century, but also because they were quiet, conventional and cautious. The Baby Boomers (1943-1960) gained their name because they were products of the fourteen year increase in birth rates worldwide after the end of World War II. Generation X (1961-1980) were the children of Baby Boomers and are considered the most apathetic and self-centered generation. Generation Y (1981-2000) was the last generation to be wholly born in the 20th Century, but the first to grow up during the start of the 21st century. Not listed in the chart is Generation Z (born starting in 2001), the first generation to be born in the 21st century.

Generation Y

Generation Y has many other titles. Howe and Straus termed them Millennials because they reported the generation itself did not want to be linked with Generation X. They described this generation in their book *Generations: The History of America's Future, 1584 to 2069* and later *Millennials Rising*. Business strategist and psychologist Don Tapscott termed them the Net Generation in his book *Growing Up Digital* because they are first generation to grow up completely in the age of the internet. This generation is also referred to as Echo Boomers because most are the children of Baby Boomers, and most were born between 1989 and 1993 when the birth rate was the highest since 1964. Other names refer to either their technological savvy in comparison to other generations or their being the first generation to grow up in the 21st century. These include Gen Y, Ygen, Generation WHY, Generation Next, Nexers, Millenniums, the Digital Generation, Google Generation, Gaming Generation, and the iGeneration. A last term is the Trophy Generation (or Trophy Kids), which describes the philosophy this generation was taught that everyone wins, no one loses, and the reward of competition is participating.

More than ever before, political candidates and those in office will need to understand and appreciate the necessity of appealing to young voters. As was the case in the 2008 presidential election, young voters have the ability to influence the outcomes of elections at the national, state and local levels. Attracting Generation Y is the most critical agenda item for both the Democratic and Republican Party. These voters will be the primary voting population in the 2012 presidential election and upcoming congressional elections, and they will have considerable influence on how their children and perhaps grandchildren vote in future elections. The following sections discuss the characteristics of Generation Y, as outlined in **Table 3.1**. The task for political candidates is to understand their demographic, social, cultural and political interests.

Table 3. 1: Profile of Generation Cohorts: G.I. Generation through Generation Y

Sources: Starks, Glenn L. "The Effect of Person-Job Fit on the Retention of Top College Graduates in Federal Agencies." *Review of Public Personnel Administration* 27 (2007): 59-70.
Johnson, Paul. *A History of the American People.* New York: Harper Collins, 1997.
Howe, Neil and William Strauss. *Generations: The History of America's Future, 1854-2069.* New York: William Morrow and Co. Inc., 1991.

	Generation Y (Millennials)	Generation X	Baby Boomers	Silent Generation	G.I. Generation
Birth Years	1981 - 2000	1961 -1980	1943-1960	1925-1942	1901-1924
Age Range, Nov. 2008	8 - 27	28 - 47	48 - 65	66 - 83	84 and over
Population (U.S. Total: 305,548,183)	83,642,525	84,542,042	67,617,596	29,626,297	6,782,196
Childhood Family Structure	Decade of the Child; overly attentive parents	Single parents; one child households; fended for themselves	Stable two-parent families	Stable two-parent families	Stable two-parent families
Parents' Jobs / Employment Experiences	Layoffs; Belief family is more important than work; mobility; independence	Layoffs; climbing corporate ladder; high divorce rates; McJobs	Secure jobs in good economic times; authority and tenure; layoffs	Great depression	Steel production; growing cities; Standard Oil and Henry Ford
Technology in Society	The Internet; Microsoft; instant communication, text messaging	Home computers; video games	Hoola-hoop; invention of television	Military, Education and Industrial Revolution	Post-industrial society
Influences	Parents; Oprah; Reality television	MTV; Bill Clinton; Bart Simpson; Jerry Seinfeld; Madonna	JFK and Jackie O; Martin Luther King, Jr.; Ozzie and Harriet; Ricky and Lucy	McArthur; Roosevelt; Stalin; Humphrey Bogart	Churchill; Theodore Roosevelt; Woodrow Wilson
Society	Fall of Soviet Union; Columbine; 9/11; globalization; sex and violence on TV and in video games	Cold War; Watergate; Fall of the Berlin Wall; Desert Storm; Women's Rights Movement; AIDS	Korean War; Vietnam War; Civil Rights Movement; Feminism; Birth Control; Start of the Space Age; Woodstock	Great depression; World War II	Prohibition; the roaring 20s; mass immigration; World War I

Generation Y Population and Cultural Characteristics

Generation Y is the most diverse generation of the 20th century, having the largest proportion of Hispanics, African Americans, and children of multi-racial parents. Political candidates must therefore understand the concerns and needs of diverse groups, as Generation Y will not only vote for candidates that espouse policies that relate to their needs but also elect tend to elect candidates that "look like them".

Table 3.2 provides population statistics for each generation as of November 2008. Generation Y comprises 27.4% of the U.S. population, only .3% smaller than Generation X which has the largest population. The next largest generation is the Baby Boomers. Generation Y is the most diverse. Over 40% of its population is comprised of minorities, with the remaining 59.3% being non-Hispanic Whites. In comparison, non-Hispanic Whites make up 65.4% of the U.S. population, 62.5% of Generation X, 74.1% of Baby Boomers, 79.5% of the Silent Generation, and 83.9% of the G.I. Generation. The majority of Generation Y minorities are Hispanic (19.0%), followed by African American (14.4%).

Generation Y is not only racially and ethnically diverse, but also socially diverse. This generation is very inclusive and accepting of different races, religions, cultures, and lifestyles. Its members are more tolerant than older generations of interracial people and couples in gay relationships. They have dated people of other races and have friends from different backgrounds. As the data in **Table 3.2** shows, many are themselves the children of interracial parents. Young Americans are also more secular than their older counterparts. They are therefore more liberal, more likely to support the Democratic Party, and less likely to support conservative government policies. At the same time, they less likely to take drugs, drink, smoke, commit crimes, and drop out of school.

Generation Y contributes significantly to the American economy. They spend approximately $200 billion annually. They generally have little or no financial commitments, spending 70% of their income arbitrarily on entertainment, travel and food. They have large disposal incomes because of their parents. Approximately 60% of couples with children under 18 are dual-earner households. An estimated 41% of teenagers between the ages of 16 and 19 have their own car, with 40% of those cars purchased by their parents. Only 23% of Generation Xers had a car when they were teenagers. Older generations, in contrast, were financially conservative and taught delayed gratification, i.e. "work now – play later" and plan for retirement instead of spending today.

Table 3.2: Population Statistics of the U.S. Population by Generation and Race/Ethnicity: November 2008

Source: U.S. Census Bureau. *Resident Population: National Population Estimates for the 2000s* (2009), http://www.census.gov/popest/national/asrh/2007-nat-res.html

Category	% U.S. Pop.	White[1]	African Ameican[1]	American Indian[1]	Asian[1]	Native Hawaiin[1]*	2 or more Races[1]	Hispanic
				Percent of Category (first column) by Race/Ethnicity				
Total U.S. Population		65.4	12.3	0.8	4.4	0.1	1.4	15.5
Generation Y	27.4	59.3	14.4	0.9	4.1	0.2	2.1	19.0
Generation X	27.7	62.5	12.5	0.7	5.6	0.2	1.1	17.5
Baby Boomers	22.1	74.1	10.7	0.7	4.1	0.1	0.8	9.5
Silent Generation	9.7	79.5	8.6	0.5	3.5	0.1	0.6	7.1
G.I. Generation	12.2	83.9	7.0	0.4	2.6	0.1	0.5	5.5

[1] Non-Hispanic
*Includes Pacific Islanders

The Education of Generation Y

Today's young Americans are the most educated in history. More attend college and they have more educational opportunities. Their educational choices include private and public schools, distance learning, and on-line education versus traditional classrooms. According to 2007 Census data, 58.5% of those 25-34 years old have completed at least one year of college. Over 58% have completed four or more years. In comparison, in 1970 only 29.8% of those in the same age group had some college education and 15.8% had completed four or more years. Since 1970, this equates to an annual increase of 0.8% completing some level of college and 0.4% completing four or more years. This increase in education is a leading contributor to an increased knowledge of political processes and political involvement. As young Americans gain more education, they gain an increased understanding of government policies, law-making processes, and how they are able to impact political decisions. In other words, they gain a greater appreciation of their political clout.

Another result of gaining higher education is an increase in income, adding to the influence of young Americans. Between 2006 and 2007, the average annual earnings for high school graduates were $31,071. For those with a Bachelor degree the average was $56,788, and it was $82,320 for those with an advanced degree. In 1976, high school graduates averaged $8,393 a year, compared to $13,033 for those with Bachelor's and $17,911 for those holding advanced degrees. Two important conclusions are reached from analyzing these income differences. First, the average incomes have increased at higher percentages for those with more education. The incomes for those who graduated high school increased by 270.2%. However, the average income for those holding a Bachelor's increased by 335.7% and 359.6% for those with an advanced degree. Second, the gap in the level of education has widened. In 1976, those with a Bachelor degree earned 55.3% more than high school graduates. Those with an advanced degree earned 37.4% more than those with a Bachelor's. In 2006, those with a Bachelor's earned 82.8% more than high school graduates and those with an advanced degree earned 45% more than those with a Bachelor's.

The gaps in incomes by sex and race are also shrinking. This can be seen, for example, when analyzing those that hold Bachelor's degrees. In 1976, men earned an average of 126.4% more than women. In 2006, the gap was still wide but had decreased to 61.2%. In 1976, Whites earned 28.5% more than African Americans. In 2006, the gap decreased to 20.9%. These higher incomes for non-White men and the closing of the income gap will require candidates to be in tune to the concerns of minorities (including women), as increasing incomes is coupled with a greater proportion of minorities in the U.S. population.

The Parents of Generation Y

Members of Generation Y admire their parents and view them as role models. This carries over in their professional lives where they value guidance and mentorship, but also desire mutual respect. This generation grew up during the "Decade of the Child" (the 1990s) when children were viewed as the center of the family. Parents talked to their kids, arranged their lives around spending time with them, and even geared family entertainment to their children. For example, television programs were given additional ratings so parents would know what programs were not suitable for their children and parents were able to block programs unsuitable for children. In 2000, 65.4% of children 6-17 years old ate dinner with their parents (Lugaila, 2000). Another 27% ate dinner with their parents at least three to six days a week. Only 3% never ate with parents. Generation Y grew up being taught by society and their parents that they could succeed, and could return home if they did not.

As children, members of other generations were to be seen and not heard (the Silent Generation) or left to fend themselves while their parents concentrated on advancing their careers (Generation X). Generation Y benefited from earlier generations wanting to make up for their and their parents' mistakes. The parents of Generation Y can be described as "active parents" or "helicopter parents", hovering over their children and providing them personal attention, constant indulgence, and protection. Some experts have said their children were overindulged and overprotected. As a result, Generation Y has respect for their parents and older people as long as they do not invade upon their independence. A survey found that children of this generation are more prone to trust their parents (86%) and teachers (86%). This is in contrast with a survey of Baby Boomers in 1974 when more than 40% said they would be better offer without their parents.

Generation Y has erased the stereotype that young people are apathetic and unengaged. Neil Howe and William Strauss (2000) characterized this generation by stating, "The Millennial Generation will entirely recast the image of youth from downbeat and alienated to upbeat and engaged – with potentially seismic consequences for America." They have benefited from the lessons of other generations. Per Lynn C. Lancaster and David Stillman (2002), "Boomers have given them the confidence to be optimistic about their ability to make things happen, and Xers have given them just enough skepticism to be cautious…if you want to remember just one key word to describe Millennials, its realistic."

Technology and Generation Y

Generation Y is the most technologically advanced. While growing up, computers were a standard fixture in most American households. To them, computers and the internet were another part of normal life. Young people stay constantly connected to the internet, and carry such devices as cell phones and personal digital assistants (PDAs) wherever they go. While older Americans used the telephone as their primary mode of communicating, Generation Y primarily uses computing and is so skilled in text messaging, chatting online, and emailing that they have created a new language comprised of abbreviated words. This generation is highly social and skilled at multitasking, using their cell phones, watching television and doing homework all at once. Almost everything they want is just a click away – information, food, and even companionship. For this reason, this generation can also be called the "Microwave Generation".

Recent studies have shown just how technologically savvy members of Generation Y are. According to a survey of 7,705 U.S. college students by Reynol and Mastrodicasa (2007):

- 97% own a computer
- 94% own a cell phone
- 76% use Instant Messaging (IM)
- 15% of IM users are logged on 24 hours a day/7 days a week
- 34% use Web sites as their primary source of news
- 28% author a blog and 44% read blogs
- 49% regularly download music and other media using peer-to-peer file sharing
- 75% have a Facebook account
- 60% own some type of portable music and/or video device such as an iPod

These statistics underscore the importance of candidates using technology as one of their primary means to reach and interact with potential young voters. Traditional methods such as sending mail or calling potential voters will not be successful in reaching young voters. President Obama used the internet and text messaging as a major part of his campaign. Future candidates must go to where young voters spend most of their time and can be easily found: cyberspace.

Generation Y Plans for the Future and Influences

Older generations planned their futures based on "traditional" values: getting married, having children, and gaining steady employment. As teenagers, members of Generation Y plan for careers, home ownership, marriage and family life. However, and unlike older generations, they don't see marriage or children as a necessity during the early part of their adult lives. They want to gain varied experiences, travel, and have fulfilling lives that are not consumed by work. They want to "work to live", not "live to work". Their personal and professional decisions are heavily influenced by their peers, community values, and through reaching consensus.

As a result of their parents' attention and influences from the media, members of Generation Y are self-confident, self-reliant, determined and optimistic. They are innovative, resourceful, competitive, and success oriented. They expect to quickly advance in their jobs, which need to be challenging, flexible, and offer monetary as well as nonmonetary rewards. While jobs will need to offer them freedom, openness, and spontaneity, Generation Y also enjoys interaction and working in teams. This generation is service oriented (rather than product oriented as previous generations), wants to make a difference at work, and is entrepreneurial. They also expect to change jobs or careers before they even start working. Just as they grew up having hundreds of choices of television stations, many shopping areas, and information at their fingertips, working-class Generation Y has the same attitude about choices in jobs. This may lead to generational clashes with employees from other generations. Older generations had a strong work ethic and loyalty to their jobs, even when they were not happy with their jobs. Often, they made careers of their first jobs. Generation Y employees may be insulted by older workers telling them what to do and how to do it because "this is how we have always done it".

Political candidates cannot hope to influence young voters simply by virtue of their positions. Older generations had patriotic and sometimes unquestioning respect for national leaders. These leaders were seen as larger than life. The idiom "You can't fight city hall" epitomized the belief that the government and government institutions were beyond reproach. Young Americans no longer espouse this sentiment. They believe the government should be held accountable when bad policies are made, political officers should be removed from office when necessary, and government institutions should be challenged when they take actions that violate citizen rights. Unlike older generations, young voters will not vote simply because of a candidate's political party, race, sex, wealth, or perceived political influence. Instead, they will support candidates that they believe can improve their daily lives and understand their concerns. For example, Generation Y is very community minded and concerned about the global impacts of their and others actions. Young people are concerned about the environment and the condition of the society they and future generations will inherit. They will support candidates with strong environmental policies and strategies to improve the general society.

Generation Y and their Society Growing Up

Generation Y grew up in a very diverse and tumultuous time. The events of September 11, 2001 changed the world and made them aware of global dangers. They then lived during wars in Iraq and Afghanistan and the overall War on Terrorism, and experienced the growing threat of nuclear proliferation from North Korea and Pakistan. They witnessed scandals in national and state governments, as well as in the private sector. The largest financial disasters in history occurred with Enron, WorldCom and other large corporations with trillions of dollars being lost. They grew up when school shootings were being perpetrated by ordinary students who felt isolated in such unexpected places as Columbine, Colorado rather than by gangs or hostile adults. They also grew up exposed to violence on television and in video games.

Generation Y also grew up when political, cultural, and economic globalization that began it the 1980s continued to make the world a much smaller place. Technology continued to be the leading catalyst for this. Advances in electronic communication such as web sharing, web conferencing, and internet social networking allowed professionals and the average person to instantaneously talk with people from almost anywhere in the world. Politically, Western nations continued to unite in their efforts to spread the principles of democracy and capitalism to non-democratic and third-world nations. These were executed through such actions as the passing of free trade agreements (such as the General Agreement on Tariffs and Trade (GATT) and the North American Free Trade Agreement (NAFTA)), global corporations, world-wide financial markets, international investments by governments and businesses, and propaganda inherently criticizing non-democratic governments. Other major variables impacting globalization have been increased immigration, global crime fighting and medical efforts, international humanitarian efforts, global pop culture (through movies and music), and increased international tourism.

The national and international impacts to the attitudes, values, and beliefs of young people must be considered by political candidates. Older generations grew up during times when the United States was relatively isolated from the rest of the world. Other nations, such as China and the Soviet Union, also isolated themselves. As a result, older generations were mistrusting of foreigners, leery of other cultures, and viewed the United States as superior to every other nation in basically every way. Young Americans understand and appreciate the importance of international cooperationalism, embrace foreign ideas, and are patriotic but value the diversity of other cultures. For these reasons, candidates will attract young voters with positions that embrace strengthening the United States through internal policies that foster domestic growth and foreign policies that foster inclusion and cooperation. This is what attracted young voters to Barack Obama.

Chapter 4: Methods to Attract Generation Y

Strategically Planning to Attract Young Voters

Attracting young voters must be part of a political party's strategic plan. It cannot be viewed as a task that comes around every four years for the general election or every two years for congressional elections. It requires candidates and political parties to use both traditional campaigning strategies through personal contacts and new strategies using electronic communication. These strategies are not mutually exclusive and must be used in combination to effectively reach Generation Y and future generations. Communication efforts, regardless of the medium, will only be effective if candidates understand youth demographics. This includes understanding the demographic segments of each generation, where these segments are located, and which are growing. Young voters should then be targeted according to their political interests. While some are concerned about policies impacting education, others are interested in programs to reduce crime in urban areas.

Attracting young voters must be viewed as a strategic effort because successfully getting young people to vote forms a habitual behavior that impacts perceptions of governmental trust. This is the key to ensuring future political party support. According to a report by Oshyn and Wang of the Century Foundation (2008), "Casting a ballot in one election profoundly increases one's propensity to vote in the next election. Even after controlling for other factors that might cause higher turnout, the researchers find that registered voters who did not vote in 1998 had a 16.6 percent chance of voting in 1999, as compared to 63.3 percent among those who voted in 1998. Moreover, the act of voting itself has an impact on perceptions of government. Some political scientists have found that the act of voting gives people a greater sense of trust in politics and political institutions."

An excerpt from a report out of the George Washington University Graduate School of Political Management (2006) referenced additional studies that found young voters will continue to vote in later elections once they are galvanized.

> Successful mobilization in one election raises people's propensity to vote in subsequent elections. Parties, candidates and interest groups should expect long-term benefits from mobilizing youth today. In one study, the authors found that 50 percent of the effect of canvassing during the 1998 New Haven (Connecticut) election persisted in 1999, even though there were no additional efforts to get out the vote. (Gerber, Green, and Shachar 2003) Another influential study (based on survey research, not experiments) found that once people begin to vote, their propensity to participate in future elections rises. (Plutzer 2002) Finally, a new study that tracked 10 canvassing experiments over time indicate that voting is habit-forming. The study found that if you get a

person to vote in one election, they will be 29 percentage points more likely to vote in the next election. (Nickerson 2004) Studies conducted in previous decades found that adults' party identification was remarkably stable over the course of their lives. If these patterns persist in the current era, then the odds are high that someone who is mobilized to vote for a particular party will continue to vote for that party for decades to come. (Sears and Levy 2003, p. 79)

The following are the strategies to attract Generation Y voters that are addressed in the remaining sections of this chapter:

- Use electronic communications such as text messaging and the internet in ways that foster dialogue
- Make personal contacts with young voters in and near locations they frequent
- Form strong alliances with voter engagement groups that target youth voters
- Tailor campaigning to different segments of the population, such as those from diverse racial and ethnic groups
- Be aware of different voter registration and Election Day procedures by state
- Begin contacting young voters as early as possible
- Use peer-to-peer contacts
- Structure political debates to be informative sessions (rather than back and forth arguments filled with blame)
- Maintain contacts with young voters after the election to keep them energized

Use the Internet

The internet and other methods of electronic communication are very effective means to reach young Americans. This is where young voters spend most of their time, and these methods are also more cost effective than using traditional methods of physically campaigning or sending mail. Over 88% of 18-29 year olds are regularly online. The web is their primary source of information and social networking. Over 41% use online social networking sites daily and 60% use them weekly. Communicating via cell phones can also be effective. Approximately 48% of young people use their mobile phone as their only telephone they are primarily used for text messaging.

Social networking web sites provide campaigners quick and easy access to millions of potential young voters from basically every demographic. Some of the most popular sites include Facebook, MySpace, MiGente, Twitter, YouTube, and BlackPlanet. A report in *Time* (Von Drehle, 2008) discussed the benefits of using such sites:

The 21st century part is this: technology makes it easier than ever to create networks and share enthusiasm. Facebook, the largest of Internet social-networking sites, boasts a market share of more than 85% of four-year U.S. universities, with millions of members averaging 20 minutes per day on-site exploring interests and keeping track of friends. Facebook has all the power of Meetup, the online campaign sensation that powered Howard Dean's brief moment in the presidential spotlight four years ago - plus much more. Its 65 billion page views per month make Facebook perfect for rapidly spreading messages and creating trends.

Candidates and political parties should adhere to the following basic guidelines when using the internet to attract Generation Y:

- Develop inviting websites (ex. colorful, use music, post interesting facts)
- Keep websites updated
- Take personal responsibility for what gets put on web pages
- Get the most out of sites by using it for varied purposes: raising funds, recruiting volunteers, and posting information
- Allow users to communicate with candidates
- Allow users to communicate and network with one another
- Allow users to get involved by helping to plan and host events, invite new members, and post profiles
- Post personal blogs to show users that candidates are personally involved with website content
- Allow users to listen to podcasts

Make Personal Contacts

Personally contacting potential voters is the most effective traditional method of increasing support, particularly with young voters (as opposed to such methods as mailings, posters, or robocalls). Although young voters are technologically savvy, they still want the opportunity for face-to-face communication when making major decisions such as choosing a political candidate. They want to personally hear what a candidate stands for and what they plan to do that will address their concerns. According to Von Drehle (2008), "Basically, it's 19th century politics using 21st century tools. The idea is rooted in a deceptively simple truth: voters are more likely to go to the polls if they are asked face-to-face by someone they trust. The rediscovery of this antique notion began in the 1990s when researchers at Yale University published several influential studies proving that personal canvassing is more effective than direct mail or phone calls from strangers."

Increased voting also results when potential voters are given practical information on voting. Green and Gerber (2004) explained that "An experiment in which high school students were taught to use a voting machine raised turnout dramatically. As Elizabeth Addonizio writes, this program increased 'the probability that an 18-year-old will vote by 19 to 24 percentage points'. Another experiment which simply reminded voters to go to the polls on Election Day and provided polling place information in New Jersey in 2003 resulted in turnout increasing by almost 14 points."

Candidates should be willing to go to young voters, rather than expect young voters to come to them. A mistake some candidates have made in the past is to hold a rally or town hall in a location removed from where young voters reside, go to school, or spend their recreational time. Rallies should be held on or near college campuses, and candidates should locate their campaign offices near college campuses or places with high densities of youth visitation such as community centers and shopping malls. Candidates must also speak at conferences that cater to young people. These include youth conferences, music conventions, and fraternity and sorority meetings. In all of these cases, young volunteers and interns should be used. Peer-to-peer networking significantly increases campaign participation and voter turnout.

When addressing young voters, candidates must address their specific concerns and tie those to the concerns of the entire population. As discussed in Chapter 2, young people have most of the same concerns as older voters. For example, during the 2008 election the general population was concerned about the economy, the wars in Iraq and Afghanistan, and rising costs. However, young and older voters had different perspectives on the impact of these issues. Older voters were concerned about how the economy was impacting their ability to pay their mortgage payments, put their children through college, and save for retirement. Young voters were worried about paying for college, starting their careers, and impacts on their day-to-day spending needs. In contrast to other Democratic and Republican candidates, Obama was better able to frame proposed solutions to these problems in a way that addressed the concerns of the general population, but also address the concerns of young voters.

In communicating with young voters, candidates need to stress cooperativeness and optimism. For example, young voters will not be swayed to support a candidate who simply preaches to them about their patriotic duty. Older generations were motivated by a sense of patriotism that sometimes overrode their personal feelings. Young voters are patriotic but still want to logically understand what they are being asked to do and why. Candidates should clearly outline plans for reaching their campaign goals in a way that gets Generation Y involved in the process, fosters teamwork, and gives them choices. Young voters want to know how they can make a difference in politics and government, and want candidates and politicians who can give them direction. Lastly, young voters will not be swayed by personal attacks by candidates or parties against each other. Negative campaigning and advertisements will be seen as a turn off. Generation Y is motivated by informative campaigning and debates that address key issues. Most are already leery of politicians who are seen as inherently corrupt and motivated by interest groups and the wealthy, and campaign attacks only feed the stereotype of corrupt politicians.

Young voter turnout increases when they are re-contacted just before the election. Green and Gerber (2001) studied the impact of contacting potential young voters just before an election to remind them to vote. Using data on telephonic and face-to-face contacts with 18-30 year old registered voters living near large public universities, they found the following:

- Phone canvassing by volunteer phone banks increased turnout by an average of 5 percentage-points
- Face-to-face canvassing increases turnout by an average of 8.5 percentage-points
- Having a peer approach them has a greater impact on voting than if a young person was contacted by a non-peer
- The more personal the connection with the potential voter, the better
- Providing voters with information about the location of their polling place makes mobilization campaigns more effective
- A purchased phone listing had a significantly larger number of incorrect phone numbers than a list compiled by students
- Two phone calls seem no more effective than a single call

They also found that direct contacts with target groups have spillover effects. They found that "for every 100 treatment subjects assigned to a canvassing campaign, 4.3 additional votes are mobilized through intended contact and 2.7 * 1.5 = 4.1 additional votes are mobilized through incidental contact. Indeed, one potential advantage of face-to-face canvassing as a mobilization tactic is that it produces substantial spillover effects."

Use Voter Engagement Groups

Non-partisan voter engagement groups and organizations are very effective in galvanizing young voters. They target specific populations of young America with unconventional contact methods, use young volunteers to reach out to their peers, and then maintain a wealth of information on youth voting habits. According to Oshyn and Wang (2008):

> Independent organizations have become vocal and visible in their efforts both to engage young adults in the electoral process and to prompt candidates to pay more attention to young voters. Most have undertaken expansive, nonpartisan, registration campaigns—focusing largely on college campuses. But some have ventured off of campuses and sent their volunteers to concerts, coffee shops, transportation hubs, and more unconventional events such as wrestling matches. Still others have dedicated resources to researching the youth voter and supplying campaigns and organizations with the best tactics for turning them out. Some organizations have become clearinghouses for information on the impact that these efforts are making on young voter turnout, tracking

turnout results and providing updated snapshots of where the young electorate stands.

The following is a list of some of the most active and successful voter engagement groups:

- Black Youth Vote www.ncbcp.org/byv
- Campus Camp Wellstone www.wellstone.org/our-programs
- Campus Compact www.compact.org
- CIRCLE www.civicyouth.org
- Declare Yourself www.declareyourself.com
- Generation Change www.generationchange.org
- Hip Hop Caucus www.hiphopcaucus.org
- Hip Hop Summit Action Network www.hsan.org
- League of Women Voters www.lwv.org
- MTV Choose or Lose! www.mtv.com/thinkmtv/chooseorlose
- The National Coalition on Black Civic Participation www.ncbcp.org
- Rock the Vote! www.rockthevote.com
- The League of Young Voters www.theleague.com
- United States Student Association www.usstudents.org
- GoVote www.govote.com

Rock the Vote! exemplifies the success of these groups. The organization uses music, pop culture (including celebrities), and the media to assist with its mission of engaging and building the political power of young people. It began in 1990 and in 1996 became the first to introduce online voter registration. During the 2008 presidential campaign, over two million young people used their website to register to vote. Its site is free to users, has no pop-up windows, and follows up with registrants to make sure they complete the registration process and know where to vote on Election Day. Text messages are sent to remind registrants to vote. The website provides polling data, voter turnout statistics, and fact sheets on young voters. It also provides information on how to mobilize young voters based upon best practices in registering, educating and boosting young voter turnout.

Because these organizations have a keen understanding of what issues are most important to young people, they provide specific and detailed information on government policies and candidate positions of interest to young people in clear terms. They provide young people the ability to engage in dialogue with one another, the organization, political candidates, and elected leaders. For example, Oshyn and Wang (2008) analyzed the use of technology by Generation Engage during the 2008 presidential election. In an effort to provide young people information, "GenGage arranges both face-to-face forums between young adults and civic leaders, as well as iChats through Apple technology. These live iChats allow young adults to connect with high-level political leaders (Nancy Pelosi and Newt Gingrich among them) in real-time conversations.

Afterward, the conversations are archived on GenGage's Web site and accessible by anyone. Recognizing the abundance of attention paid to young adults in college, GenGage is targeting its efforts to the 49 percent of young adults who have never attended college."

These groups do not only target college students, but recognize the importance of getting non-college graduates involved in voting. For example, Black Youth Vote (BYV) has been primarily organizing youth voters in the South for over a decade. Part of their target population is high school dropouts. They target movie theaters, shopping malls, night clubs, sporting events, and even bus stops and subway stations. According to an article by Rizga (2008), the national coordinator of BYV, Jordan Thierry, believes "Youth organizers need to spend more time and money on reaching non-college youth, because current disparity gives white and upper-middle class youth and their issues priority on the agenda, further discouraging non-college youth from participating."

The same article discusses how the League of Young Voters targets low-income and minority youth by combining traditional voter organizing tactics, such as canvassing, with new methods to increase young voter turnout. The League uses Street Teams who post fliers and stickers in clubs, coffee shops and community based organizations. They also used a "balanced mixture of new mediums -- including MySpace, Facebook, YouTube, and text messaging in order to reach the widest number of youths from varying backgrounds. While most youth groups use Facebook as their online organizing destination, the immigrant marches in 2006 revealed that Latino youth still prefer MySpace and text messaging. Most of Black Youth Vote members also use MySpace."

These groups also target community college students because they still live in their hometowns and provide a link to other students and young people in their communities who didn't attend college. The League, BYV, Voto Latino, Youth People For (YP4), and College Democrats of America (CDA) have all expanded their youth target populations to community colleges.

Attracting Young Voters from Different Ethnic Groups

Even though Generation Y is generally homogenous in their beliefs and experiences, there are some subtle differences in segments of the population. For this reason, members of different races and ethnicities may require additional methods of being targeted to increase their voter turnout rates. For example, large populations of African American youth can be found in urban areas. Urbanites listen to different types of music, shop and hang out in different areas, are more dispersed (for example, not clustered on college campuses), and are more concerned about day-to-day survival than long-term issues such as the environment. Children of middle- and upper-class families living in suburban areas are concerned about giving back, jobs that offer careers, the environment, and long-term issues that will help them buy homes and raise families in the future. Higher percentages of Hispanic youth are in Florida, New Mexico and Colorado. One of their primary concerns is immigration laws that may impact them or members of their family.

Although their concerns are different, youth from different racial and ethnic backgrounds respond positively to the same types of voter engagement tactics. First, they each should be targeted through social networking techniques that target the types of music they listen to, recreational and community activities they engage in, and places they enjoy spending their spare time. Second, the most effective way to interact with them is through their peers. Minority youth are more prone to show interest when interacting with people of the same age and race or ethnicity. Third, they like other members of their age group can be reached through emails and text messaging. These groups spend a lot of time online and using their cell phones.

Potential young voters in ethnic and immigrant communities should be targeted as young as possible. They are easy to reach, more likely to speak English than their parents, and can then politically educate other members of their communities. CIRCLE outlined the findings of two studies in recommending the following:

> When working in ethnic or immigrant communities, be sure to ask all voters you contact to volunteer to reach out to their neighbors: research also indicates that in ethnic and immigrant communities the most trusted messenger is someone who looks like the potential voter. (Michelson 2004)

> This is the case with most voters, but even more so in these communities. Also, youth are at least as easy to reach as older voters. Latino 18-29 year olds are easier to reach than those in the 30-39 age range and the same as 40-59 year old Latinos. For Asians, young voters were less likely to be contacted than the older Asian-American voters but as easy to contact as those in the 30-49 age ranges. (Ramírez and Wong 2006)

How State Voter Registration Techniques Improve Voter Turnout

Research shows that the election process in each state has a significant impact on young voter turnout. Most states have a standard process. Voters are required to register by a specified date in advance of Election Day. Voting then takes place during specified hours on Election Day at designated polling places, and absentee ballots are only allowed under specific circumstances and are due on a specified date before Election Day. However, some states have alternative methods for voter registration and actual voting, and research has shown that these increase the turnout rates of voters. Youth turnout rates particularly increase as a result. These methods include allowing registration up to and on Election Day, unrestricted absentee voting, voting outside of precinct-based polling places, vote-by-mail, voting centers, and early in-person voting.

Turnout is further improved by voters being mailed sample ballots, directions to polling places, and other registration and voting instructions. Research has shown that young people are more likely to vote when personally contacted. During the 2000 election in states that mailed sample ballots, the turnout rate was 7 percentage points among 18-24 year old registered voters. In states that mailed ballots, outlined polling place location information, and offered extended polling hours on Election Day, the turnout rate was 10 percentage points higher among 18-24 year olds in 2000.

These alternative methods decrease the cost of voting to states and localities, and to the voters themselves. For example, early voting gives voters more time to cast their ballot versus waiting for Election Day. Jamison, Shin and Day (2002) found that young voters in the 2000 election were more likely to report they did not vote because the polling hours conflicted with their school or work schedules. These methods make the voting process more efficient for jurisdictions and reduce the volume of people turning out to vote on Election Day. Texas has allowed early voting since 1987 and its use by voters has increased each election ever since.

Various methods are used by different states (see **Table 4.1**). North Dakota is the only state that does not require voter registration. Every other state allows voter registration at the Department of Motor Vehicles and registration by mail. Oregon is the only state that allows vote-by-mail and has done so since 1981. Voter turnout in the 2000 presidential election was 79.8% and was 86.5% in 2004. Colorado has used voting centers since 2003. Voting centers provide polling places in large, strategically located places. Some jurisdictions in Louisiana, Texas and Delaware have weekend voting. Another option is designating Election Day as a Holiday. Currently, nine states allow this. Maryland has observed it as a holiday since 1882 and Illinois since 1943.

In states with Election Day registration, political parties are more likely to contact potential voters and young people are more likely to vote. On average, the likelihood of young voters being contacted by a political party is 11 percentage points higher than in states that do not allow this. According to research by Kirby, Linkins, and Glennon (2008), the youth turnout rate is on average 14 percentage points higher during presidential elections in states that have Election Day registration. The following states offer Election Day registration:

- Idaho
- Maine
- Minnesota
- Montana
- New Hampshire
- Oregon
- Rhode Island
- Wisconsin
- Wyoming

States are using alternative methods to increase voter registration. For example, California sends birthday style voter registration cards to every citizen that turns 18 and that is issued a California driver's license or identification card.

This is part of the California Secretary of State's Birthday Card Program that began in 1999. An estimated 400,000 cards are mailed annually.

All of the aforementioned methods have been shown to increase voter turnout. However, youth voter turnout is also impacted by voter demographics, the candidates running for office, local political traditions, and socio-economic issues. Fitzgerald (2003) conducted an analysis of how several independent variables impact youth voter turnout. These variables fell under the categories of electoral competitiveness, voter mobilization, individual voter characteristics, and the voting legal structure (i.e. registration and voting process in states) during the presidential election years from 1972 through 2000. She found a significant statistical relationship between Election Day registration and mail balloting on youth voter turnout. Election Day registration increased the probability of youth voter turnout by 14 percentage points and voting by mail increased the probability by 40 percentage points. Strong party loyalty (or strong partisanship) and being contacted by a political party also had a significant relationship and increased the probability by 13 percentage points and 22 percentage points, respectively. The probability of voting was higher for young voters with high incomes (5 percentage points) and high education levels (28 percentage points). The probability was negatively impacted for youth voters who were unemployed (-6 percentage points), African American (-2 percentage points), and from Southern states (-8 percentage points).

Pop Culture and Youth Voting

Because young people are so in tune with modern culture through technology and civic engagement, it is not surprising that their political engagement is heavily influenced by pop culture. Musicians, artists, actors, producers and other members of the entertainment community have taken an active and aggressive role in developing strategies to increase young voter turnout. They have integrated voting into concerts, public service announcement, talk show appearances, and personal appearances in addition to sponsoring activities with the sole purpose of getting young people involved in politics. Some have even established organizations that strive to increase young voter turnout. The key to their strategies are providing political information through websites, holding events, establishing peer networks, and building coalitions among voter engagement groups and organizations.

Table 4.1: Election Process in each State

Source: United States Election Assistance Commission, www.eac.gov

	No Voter Registration	Mail Registration	Motor Vehicle Registration	Election Day Registration	Unrestricted Absentee Voting	In-person Early Voting	Vote by Mail	Extended Polling Hours	Weekend Voting	Election Day is a Holiday
Alabama		Y	Y							
Alaska		Y	Y		Y	Y				
Arizona		Y	Y		Y	Y				
Arkansas		Y	Y		Y	Y				
California		Y	Y		Y					
Colorado		Y	Y		Y	Y				
Connecticut		Y	Y							Y
Delaware		Y	Y							
Florida		Y	Y							
Georgia		Y	Y							
Hawaii		Y	Y		Y	Y				Y
Idaho		Y	Y	Y	Y	Y				
Illinois		Y	Y							Y
Indiana		Y	Y							Y
Iowa		Y	Y		Y	Y				
Kansas		Y	Y		Y	Y				
Kentucky		Y	Y							
Louisiana		Y	Y		Y					Y
Maine		Y	Y	Y						
Maryland		Y	Y							Y
Massachusetts		Y	Y							
Michigan		Y	Y							
Minnesota		Y	Y	Y						
Mississippi		Y	Y							
Missouri		Y	Y							
Montana		Y	Y		Y	Y				Y
Nebraska		Y	Y		Y	Y				
Nevada		Y	Y		Y	Y				
New Hampshire		Y	Y	Y						
New Jersey		Y	Y							
New Mexico		Y	Y		Y	Y				Y

New York		Y	Y				
North Carolina		Y	Y		Y	Y	
North Dakota	Y				Y		
Ohio		Y	Y		Y		
Oklahoma		Y	Y		Y	Y	
Oregon		Y	Y	Y			Y
Pennsylvania		Y	Y				
Rhode Island		Y	Y				
South Carolina		Y	Y				
South Dakota		Y	Y				
Tennessee		Y	Y			Y	
Texas		Y	Y			Y	
Utah		Y	Y		Y		
Vermont		Y	Y		Y	Y	
Virginia		Y	Y		Y		
Washington		Y	Y		Y		
West Virginia		Y	Y	Y				Y
Wisconsin		Y	Y	Y	Y		
Wyoming		Y	Y		Y		

The spectrum of entertainment forums that have gotten involved in influencing young voters include music and sports outlets. They range from MTV to professional wrestling. MTV launched its Chose or Lose campaign in 1991 and sweeps the nation each general election year with a tour bus that stops at college campuses. Using a combination of voter information and entertainment, their efforts have led to thousands of registered voters and students getting involved in politics. They have enlisted the support and crowd draw from such pop icons as Kanye West, Christina Aguilera, and Justin Timberlake. The WWE began its "Smackdown Your Vote!" campaign in 2000. Using the popularity of its wrestlers, the organization sponsors events nationwide to get young people involved in voting using non-partisan methods. The Republican Party has registered new voters at NASCAR races. President George W. Bush attended the Daytona 500 in 2004 and a voter registration booth was set up at the event.

Rock the Vote!, based in Washington, D.C., has worked to get youth involved in voting since it was founded 1990. Since that time, it has used celebrities in public service announcements to stress the importance of registering and voting on such television networks as Fox, MTV, BET, and VH-1. These have included Tom Cruise, Justin Timberlake, Samuel Jackson, Ricky Martin, Whoopi Goldberg, Leonardo DiCaprio, Madonna, Macy Gray, The Ramones, and Chris Connell. The organization has also been a primary supporter of federal legislation to increase youth registration. In 1991 it aggressive supported the National Voter Registration Reform Act which was passed in 1993 and required states to allow voter registration when an eligible citizen applies for or renews a driver's license. The Act (also called the "Motor Voter" bill) was vetoed by President George H.W. Bush but signed into law by President Clinton. President Clinton highlighted Rock the Vote!'s role in getting the bill passed. The law went into effect in 1995 and also requires states to designate voter registration agencies, mandates first time voters to vote in person, and established criminal penalties for anymore who manipulates the registration or voting process. One year after the law was passed, 40% of new registrants were under 30.

The Hip-Hop Summit Action Network (HSAN) was founded in 2001. Per the organization's website (www.hsan.org), HSAN is dedicated to harnessing the cultural relevance of Hip-Hop music to serve as a catalyst for education advocacy and other societal concerns fundamental to the empowerment of youth. HSAN is a non-profit, non-partisan national coalition of Hip-Hop artists, entertainment industry leaders, education advocates, civil rights proponents, and youth leaders united in the belief that Hip-Hop is an enormously influential agent for social change which must be responsibly and proactively utilized to fight the war on poverty and injustice. Russell Simmons (Chairman of HSAN), Sean "Diddy" Combs, Jermaine Dupri, Ciara, Wyclef Jean, Reverend Run of Run DMC, Eminem, Beyonce Knowles, and Will Smith are just some of the celebrities that have hosted, spoken or performed at major events. The organization has held major events around the country to increase youth voter participation, but particularly African American and Hispanic youths.

Although organizations such as Rock the Vote! and HSAN espouse to be non-partisan, many of the pop culture individuals that support them or speak on their own are not. Some have gotten very active in persuading young voters to support the same political candidate or party as they do. For example, during the 2004 presidential election Ricky Martin, Clint Black, Poison, Kid Rock, Reba McIntyre, Britney Spears, and Wayne Newton were vocal supporters of the Republican Party and the re-election of President George W. Bush.

Supporters of the Democratic Party included Leonardo DiCaprio, Julia Roberts, and Green Day. Bruce Springsteen, REM, Pearl Jam, the Dixie Chicks, Jackson Browne, Bonnie Raitt, Kenny "Babyface" Edmonds, Ben Harper, James Taylor, John Mellencamp and other artists participated in a national concert tour in September - October 2004 called "Vote for Change" held in key swing states to rally support for John Kerry and denounce the possible re-election of President Bush. Concerts were held in Arizona, Florida, Iowa, Michigan, Missouri, New Jersey, Ohio, Pennsylvania, Washington, and Washington, D.C.

Beyond musicians and actors speaking and giving concerts, Hollywood has also had an impact on politics. President Bush has been perhaps one of the most negatively portrayed past President in movies. In movies such as Oliver Stone's "W" and Michael Moore's "Fahrenheit 9/11" he was portrayed as an alcohol abuser and womanizer, and an alleged connection was depicted between his family and the bin Laden family. Documentaries such as Spike Lee's "When the Levees Broke" exemplified the Bush's administrations lack of response to the devastation immediately after Hurricane Katrina. The depiction of Bush and other candidates in such movies impact the perceptions of voters. It may be especially damaging when movie goers cannot distinguish fact from fiction.

Chapter 5: The Democratic and Republican Parties

Challenges Political Parties Face

The greatest challenge for political parties over the coming decades will be not only to increase their ranks with young voters but also to build a sense of stalwart support in these members. As was the case in recent presidential elections, young people may identify with one party but vote for candidates from another based on their attraction to candidates rather than totally by party loyalty. One reason this occurred in the past is because some candidates strayed away from the basic tenants of their parties. Voters thus voted for the candidates who they believed would support their positions, even if that candidate was from a different party. Another reason is that candidates from the same party differed in their stance on the same issues. This resulted in disjointed party loyalty and distrust among voters over single party choices. Finally, young voters are not as trusting of political candidates and political parties. Those that become disenfranchised may switch parties or not vote at all.

The above issues necessitate radical changes by political parties. Parties will have to establish political platforms based upon agreement on key issues across the party (from liberals to conservatives) and candidates must exhibit loyalty to this platform in the policies they support. Political parties and candidates will also have to change how they attempt to attract voters and realize young voters have very different viewpoints toward politics than previous generations. Baby Boomers and older generations are ideologically different. They are patriotic and grew up in times that instilled in them a sense of civic duty. They were more trusting of national leaders to guide them through such events as the Great Depression, world wars, the Cold War, and recessions. Young Americans are patriotic but not as trusting of national leaders.

Attracting young voters is not only critical for political parties during a current election, but also to build long-term support. A primary task for parties is attracting first time voters. Studies show that political party loyalty begins with young adults, and they predominantly remain loyal to the first party they become affiliated with. According to Oshyn and Wang (2008),

> A report by Young Voter Strategies outlines data indicating that 'party identification develops in early adulthood', after which point, a person's party identification generally remains consistent for the rest of his or her life. The report asserts that people under the age of thirty generally are still forming their political beliefs, which leaves them more open to outreach by political parties than their older counterparts. The degree of stability in party loyalty was drawn from studies done that questioned voters on which party they supported in their first presidential election and which party they supported at the time of the interview for the study. The report states that 'of those who can remember their vote for President two-thirds still identify with the same

party they first voted for'. Furthermore, over half (56 percent) of these presidential voters had never crossed party lines.

These findings signal concern for the Republican Party. In the 2008 election, half (50%) of young respondents identified themselves as Democrat, compared to 29% Republican and 12% Independent according to a poll by Rock the Vote!. This was compared to 40% of young adults identifying themselves as Democrat in 2006, 30% Republican and 23% as Independent. Those in 2008 included a large number of new voters. If most of these voters actually do stay loyal to the Democratic Party, the Republican Party must devise strong tactics to lure some young voters away from the Democratic Party or to attract first-time voters in coming elections. After the 2008 election, the Republican Party found that it had not only lost the presidential race, but also majority control of both Houses of Congress. Its leaders immediately began analyzing how it lost support and what it needed to do to regain popularity. A top priority was developing strategies to increase support from minorities and young voters. These were the two demographics that overwhelmingly supported the Democratic Party in the last three elections, particularly in the 2008 presidential race.

Ideological Differences between the Democratic and Republican Parties

While other parties exist (ex. the Green Party and Libertarian Party), the Democratic and Republican Parties remain the two dominant American political parties. **Table 5.1** outlines the basic ideologies of each. These are general ideologies because the beliefs of members from each party range from very liberal to very conservative. For example, while Democrats generally support abortion there are conservative Democrats who are in strong opposition. Support for a political party may also change due to the state of the nation's economic, social or international environment. For example, in bad economic conditions such as recessions voters may support Democratic candidates because voters want government action to set fiscal policy to stimulate the economy. When the government proposes unpopular social programs that will be paid through raising income taxes, the Republican Party gains more support. The political ideologies of each party have changed over the years, leading some voters to become disenfranchised with the party they have ideologically supported and an increase in the number of voters who consider themselves Independent.

The ideologies of the Democratic Party outlined in **Table 5.1** are more in line with the ideologies of Generation Y than the Republican Party. Young adults are generally liberal and support government programs that improve social welfare and the environment. They support government programs to improve education, and are in favor of government economic programs that support workers rather than predominantly big businesses. They favor U.S. international cooperation rather than solitary action, are in favor of same-sex marriage, and support the government working for and with the people rather than taking a more authoritative role. Young voters also do not support recent Republican Party presidents' policies that interfered with the personal sovereignty of people and other nations. They are against the government seeking to tell people what to do and how to live. For example, Republican politicians have sought to set laws against abortion and gay marriage. These are seen as non-government affairs and issues of personal choice. Some past Republican presidents, particularly George W. Bush, exercised "cowboy diplomacy" by using force against nations that were deemed enemies of democracy rather than diplomacy and cooperation with the United Nations and allied nations.

Young voters also support the Democratic Party because of their diversity. Because Generation Y is the most diverse in history, they support the Democratic Party's ideology of support to women and minorities.

Because of the congruency of Generation Y beliefs and the Democratic Party's ideology, the Republican Party has two primary challenges. First, it will have to take a more mainstream and less conservative stance on key issues to attract young supporters. Scott Keeter, public opinion survey expert with the Washington-based Pew Research Center, described how young Americans are the most diverse and liberal in history: "They are very tolerant of interracial dating. They don't have hang-ups about gay marriage. They are welcoming to immigrants, more so than other age groups. All of this, I think, makes them very distinctive and points to the fact that they are less supportive of the Republican Party, which is much more the socially conservative party in the U.S." (Franceschi, 2008)

Second, it must find strong to leaders who have the ability to develop a vision that attracts young voters while not losing the supporters it already has. McCain and Palin attempted to do this in the 2008 election by describing themselves as "mavericks" that supported Republican ideology but would take a more progressive stance in governing. They lost the election primarily because they failed to distance themselves from the past mistakes of the Party, but they were also perceived to espouse a more conservative Republican ideology. For example, Palin was against abortion and McCain was not in favor of government economic intervention with the private market during a serious economic downturn.

While the Republican Party is generally struggling with trying to maintain a conservative ideology at a time when the mainstream attitude is generally liberal, it is also trying to maintain unity with its existing members. For example, no Republican Senators and only three Republicans in the House of Representatives voted for passing the 2009 stimulus bill. However, many Republican governors supported the bill and accepted government funds to augment their state budgets. Long-term Republican Senator Arlen Specter shocked the political world in April 2009 when he switched from the Republican to the Democratic Party. He stated the Republican Party was at odds with his principles. He further stated that "As the Republican Party has moved farther and farther to the right, I have found myself increasingly at odds with the Republican philosophy and more in line with the philosophy of the Democratic Party... In the course of the last several months ... I have traveled the state and surveyed the sentiments of the Republican Party in Pennsylvania and public

Table 5.1: Basic Ideological Differences Between the Democratic and Republican Party

Source: Starks, Glenn L. and F. Erik Brooks. *How Your Government Works: A Topical Encyclopedia of the Federal Government.* Westport, Connecticut: Greenwood Press, 2008.

When considering...	Democrats are generally...	Republicans are generally...
Basic ideology	Liberal	Conservative
Legalized Abortion	For (Pro-choice)	Against (Pro-life)
Tax Cuts	In favor to support lower income Americans	In favor of cuts for the wealthy
Role of the government	In favor of a less authoritative government	In favor of a more authoritative government
Government regulation of business	In favor of more regulation	In favor of less regulation
Government spending for social programs	Supportive of more assistance to the poor and middle class	In favor of citizens supporting themselves
Environmentalism	In favor of stricter laws	Opposed to stricter laws
Affirmative Action	In favor of laws supporting	Opposed to laws supporting
Gun Control	In favor of more laws	Opposed to laws as violating 2nd Amendment
Health Care	In favor of universal care	In favor of HMOs
Education	In favor or more federal spending	In favor of less federal spending
Foreign policy	In favor of U.S. involvement through the United Nations	In favor of direct U.S. involvement
Minorities	Comprised of more minorities	Comprised of fewer minorities
Sex	Comprised of more women	Comprised of more men
Same-sex Unions	In favor	Opposed
Minimum wage increases	In favor because it helps workers prosper	Opposed because it puts a burden on businesses

opinion polls, observed other public opinion polls and have found that the prospects for winning a Republican primary are bleak." (CNN, 2009) Specter's move not only further hurt the stability and reputation of the Republican Party but also increased the Democratic Party's control of the Senate.

Meghan McCain, daughter of Senator John McCain, also caused controversy when she proclaimed the Republican Party was having a political civil war. The war was resulting from a battle between the past and the future – older conservative Republicans against young progressive members. Her comments resulted from her frustration with what she perceived as an overly partisan and divisive party, and a fear of its older members to face their fears of the world changing.

If the Republican Party continues to lose voter support and have factions within its membership, it will continue to lose members to the Democratic Party and there is a possibility that strong conservatives in this nation could eventually represent a third political party.

What the Democratic and Republican Parties Need to Do

In an effort to rejuvenate their parties and grow their memberships, both Parties appointed new leaders to run their national conventions after the 2008 general election. Tim Kaine was appointed the Democratic National Committee (DNC) Chairman. Kaine was chosen because of his support for President Obama's policies, and also because the party believed he could engage citizens civically. Michael Steele was appointed the Republican National Committee (RNC) Chairman, the first African American to hold that post. One of his possible appeals will be bringing more African Americans to the party. The Republican Party is also deciding on candidates for the 2012 presidential election. On February 27, 2009, conservative Republicans chose Massachusetts Governor Mitt Romney as the leading contender. Part of the party continues to hope it can revive enough conservative activism in the United States to win congressional and presidential control of the government. The two fallacies in their strategies are that they are relying on extreme criticism of President Obama's strategies that border on scare tactics to influence voters and, second, they neglect the more liberal viewpoints of young voters.

Although the Democratic Party captured the largest percentage of youth votes in 2008 and 2004, the Republican Party has been popular with young voters in the past. David Frum (2008) commented on how the Republican Party had the greatest share of the youth vote in 1984 and 1988 due to the popularity of Ronald Reagan. Reagan captured 59% of the youth vote in 1984 and Bush captured 52% of their vote in 1988, although Bush benefited from Reagan's popularity. According to Frum, between 1988 and 2008 the Republican Party "lost its connection to the young, and the problem gets worse with every passing election. Today's twentysomethings are the most anti-Republican age group in the electorate." He attributes this to four challenges facing the party:

1. Young people react to the success or failure of the first politicians they know. The twentysomethings of the 1980s, for example, associated the Democratic Party with the malaise of Jimmy Carter — and the GOP with the triumphs of Ronald Reagan. Today's Republican Party is associated with a wave of disappointments and embarrassments: Iraq, Hurricane Katrina, congressional corruption scandals, the mortgage crisis.

2. The Reagan years were a time of prosperity for young workers. Unemployment plunged, wages rose, housing became more affordable. The Bush years have not been so favorable. The cost of a college degree rose faster than pay for college graduates. New college graduates saw their wages actually drop after inflation. And the costs of housing have outpaced incomes for just about all young people.

3. The Republican Party has become increasingly identified with conservative Christianity. Younger Americans are becoming more secular and more permissive. In particular, young Americans have become increasingly tolerant of homosexuality and increasingly willing to have children outside marriage. While unmarried births have dropped among teenagers since the welfare reform of 1995, unmarried births have actually been rising among women in their 20s.

4. Today's twentysomethings are browner and blacker than those of the 1980s. Hispanics and Asians both tilt strongly Democratic, as of course do African-Americans.

Frum outlines a "plan of action" for the party to regain young supporters. This includes allowing social security taxes to be deductable on tax returns; presenting a "sunnier face on social issues" such explaining ending *Roe v. Wade* does not mean individual states have to ban abortion; reemphasizing environmental policies; and capitalizing on the Bush administration's success in the United States not experiencing a terror attack since September 11, 2001.

The issues for the Republican Party to address to attract voters are not different than those required of the Democratic Party. Supporters of each party have the same concerns. For example, during the 2008 presidential election the top issues among young voters supporting both parties were the economy, immigration, gas prices, health care, and the federal budget. The key to attracting young voters is how candidates and each party frame their approaches to tackling these issues. For example, a conservative approach to dealing with the economy would be for no or very little government intervention with businesses. A liberal approach would be for the government to heavily invest in the economy and to control free market activity. A middle of the road approach would be for the government to intervene in markets threatening the nation's economic stability through loans (rather than grants), provide oversight, and then allow the market room to recover without overly burdensome government control. Candidates and parties have to understand how the majority of voters believe the best approach would be. This information can be obtained through polls, town hall meetings, and other survey techniques.

The following recommendations for political parties to attract young voters are especially targeted to the Republican Party, but are also required of the Democratic Party.

- Build a unified political party platform based upon a strategic vision that stresses inclusiveness and equality
- Espouse a mild stance on issues versus strongly and devoutly conservative or liberal stances
- Support limited government interference with private industry unless a crisis situation necessitates government intervention
- Adopt responsible fiscal policy that maintains the foundation of a sound economy
- Support an open government versus government based on closed policies and secrecy
- Practice strong national leadership
- Use of straight talk from candidates versus catchy phrases and jargon (ex. "maverick" and "Joe Six-pack")
- End negative campaigning and slanderous attacks against opponents
- Stick to recommendations based on facts instead of hollow promises (ex. "Read my lips, no new taxes"), and make no promises that are outside of the President's ability (ex. promising to pass laws – only Congress can pass laws)
- Develop fiscal policy that supports the lower and middle class and not just the wealthy
- Institute programs that get citizens involved, such as volunteer programs that support federal programs
- Institute policies that will ensure social justice
- Encourage people to act versus attempting to force them to behave in a certain manner
- Address the needs of different segments of the population
- Develop policies that support international cooperation and diplomacy versus solitary U.S. decisions
- Focus on better domestic policy and support of citizens
- Develop policies that lead to a leaner, more efficient, effective and organized government
- Support a strong national defense

Chapter 6: Impact of the 2008 Election on Future Elections

The 2008 general election exemplified the power of democracy when citizens are rejuvenated to get involved in the political process. The economic and political environments of the nation drove citizens to the polls to demand change and the recognition of their concerns by government leaders. The possibility of making history with the nation's first African American president added to the rejuvenation of voters. This last factor was one of the primary symbols of change that galvanized young voters. Another was a candidate young voters could relate to and believe in to bring about the change they wanted.

The Republican Party lost the presidency and congressional seats for the opposite reason. The party and its members lost touch with the concerns of mainstream America, held onto to an outdated platform that supported a small fraction of the American population, and supported unpopular policies through justifications that they were acting in everyone's best interests. While it should not be questioned that Republican leaders believed they were acting in the best interest of the country, what can be questioned is their tactics and ignoring of popular opinion.

The outcome of the 2008 election has forever changed American politics in two important ways. First and foremost, it has solidified the idea of the American dream. It has proven that any person can achieve high positions in government (including the very highest) without regard to race, sex, or economic background. While racism and sexism still remains in the United States, the outcome of the election shows the historical vestiges of bigotry are diminishing and the general population has embraced beliefs in equality and equal opportunity. Second, the election ended a disturbing trend in American politics that had existed for decades: the ignorance of the political concerns of the general population in favor of the rich, big business, and powerful lobbyists. This was particularly the practices of politicians in the 1980s and 1990s. It is the primary reason young voters became disengaged in voting. But the late 1990s and early 2000s ushered in a new era of understanding that change could occur through political mobilization. This was the same understanding used by women to gain the right to vote in the 1920s. Civil rights leaders understood this in the 1960s when Martin Luther King Jr. used national awareness to drive government action. The gay and lesbian community used this same practice to gain rights at the state level and to strive for the same rights at the federal level. However, the 2008 election created change at the national and perhaps international level by voters rallying for cultural, social, economic, and political change through voting.

Obama's popularity with young people will be a major political obstacle for Republican candidates. Most of his young supporters will vote again in the 2012 general election and another influx of young voters will become eligible to vote for the first time. The task for the Democratic Party is to hold on to their current supporters, and continue to implement strategies to attract first time young voters. The task for the Republican Party is more challenging. It must develop strategies to attract young voters away from the Democratic Party and also attract new young voters. These efforts must be employed by both parties by their national conventions leaders, and also presidential and congressional incumbents and candidates. Each party must also establish political partisanship with the other and unity within their own parties.

Young people voting, their involvement in the political process and their involvement in government are critical to ensuring our democracy represents our population and also in ensuring the future of our national government. Whether young voters support the Democratic or Republican Party, it is critical that they get involved in the political process. This underlines the importance of non-partisan voter engagement groups remaining strong entities that get young voters registered to vote and continue to push for high young voter turnout. The government must take a more active role in supporting these organizations.

The next two sections outline two areas that will be important for political parties to integrate into their campaigns for future elections: using the internet to attract new voters and communicate with citizens, and attracting uneducated potential young voters.

Use of the Internet to Attract Voters and Communicate with Citizens

The internet will continue play a major role in governance and in influencing voters of all ages. With technological advancements, it may become the primary means of communicating with the electorate in coming general elections. President Obama used the internet as a major part of his 2008 campaign and he has continued to use it during his administration. He exemplified its importance in a speech given in 2008:

> And we'll use technology to connect people to service more extensively and effectively. We turn to websites like craigslist to find apartments and jobs. So we'll expand USA Freedom Corps to create an online network where Americans can browse opportunities to volunteer. You'll be able to search by category, time commitment, and skill sets; you'll be able to rate service opportunities, build service networks, and create your own service pages to track your hours and activities. This will empower more Americans to craft their own service agenda, and make their own change from the bottom up.

An article by Pew Internet and American Life Project (2008) discussed how voters will continue to expect the internet to play a major role during the Obama administration. Their research was based on a survey of those who used the internet in connection with the 2008 general election. They found that those of different sexes, races, education levels, and annual incomes use the internet at basically the same rate to gain information on the presidential transition. The only exception is that young voters used the internet more. Per the results of a survey of 2,254 adults they conducted:

- 62% of Obama voters expect that they will ask others to support the policies of the new administration over the next year. Among Obama voters who were engaged online during the campaign, 25% expect to support the administration's agenda by reaching out to others online.

- 46% of Obama voters and 33% of McCain voters expect to hear directly from their candidate or party leaders over the next year. Fully 51% of online Obama supporters expect some kind of ongoing communication from the new administration—34% of Obama-supporting email users expect email communication, 37% of social network site users expect SNS updates, and 11% of phone texters expect to receive text messages from the new administration.

- 27% of wired (online) Obama voters have gone online to learn about or get involved with the presidential transition process. Nine percent of online McCain voters have visited websites hoping to rebuild the GOP or elect conservative candidates in the future.

- 37% of Obama voters who use social networking sites expect to receive updates from the administration on these sites. Most expect to receive these updates on either a weekly (12%) or monthly (11%) basis, while 14% expect them to occur less frequently.

- 34% of Obama voters who use email expect to hear from the new administration via email. One in ten (10%) expect to receive these email contacts on a weekly basis, and 9% expect to do so monthly.

- 38% of all Obama voters expect to hear from the administration via mail. Some 7% expect to receive mail from the new administration on a weekly basis and 12% expect to do so monthly, while 19% expect to be contacted by mail just a few times a year.

- 17% of all Obama voters expect to receive phone calls from the new administration at least occasionally. Just 2% expect to receive phone calls on a weekly basis, and most (10%) would prefer these communications to take place a few times a year.

- 11% of Obama voters who own cell phones and use text messaging expect to be contacted by text messaging, with most (6%) preferring that these text message contacts occur less than once a month.

Attracting Uneducated Young Voters

The primary challenge for political parties and candidates is to develop strategies to increase the engagement of potential young voters who have not attended college. The majority of young voters are those that have obtained some level of college education. Those with no college attendance continue to have low turnout rates (see **Table 6.1**). In 2004, 59% of those 18-24 year olds who had some college education voted in the general election. This was compared to 61% of those 18-29 and 77.5% of those 30 and older. These rates were lower than those in the 1970s but higher than in 1996 and 2000. In comparison, the rates for those with no college education were much lower. In 2004, only 33.7% of 18-24 year olds with no college education cast ballots. The same percentage of those 18-29 year old s voted and 56.1% of those 30 and older. The statistics are just as concerning when analyzing primary voting. While one in every four college-students 18-25 voter during Super Tuesday, only one in fourteen non-college youth voted.

Those that have not attended college have the greatest stake in politics yet do not exercise their political power. Consider the primary issues for young people in the 2008 election. The wars in the Middle East (Iraq and Afghanistan) have the greatest impact on non-college youths because they are more likely to join the military. They are also most likely to not be Officers, and thus face serving on the front lines of wars and major contingencies. The economy was also a major issue. Job losses, rising gas prices, and inflation has the greatest negative impact on those from lower incomes who are those without college educations. This group will also require the greatest amount of government assistance in the form of social welfare programs, improved health care programs, and government assistance in finding work.

Per an article in Wiretap (Rizga, 2008), "There are close to 13 million 18- to 25-year-olds, who have never been enrolled in college in America. So far only about three million voted in the primaries. These non-college youths come disproportionately from lower-income backgrounds and African American and Latino communities. It is these very communities that stand to gain the most from more political power and resources, especially during the current recession." Those that have not attended college are more concerned on day-to-day living. Their concerns include escaping from poverty, jobs, community programs for the youth, sports programs in their schools, financial aid to attend college, and protection from gangs and police harassment. This group suffers the most from racial prejudice, environmental neglect, social and economic neglect and oppression, economic exploitation, crime, police brutality, and government support apathy. They are predominantly African American and Hispanic, and live predominantly in urban cities.

If political parties and candidates could galvanize this group, these voters would become a powerful force in influencing government policies in almost every realm of public policy and administration. The primary challenges are that they are hard to reach physically and psychologically. They are not centrally located on a college campus. Some in urban areas live in neighborhoods that voter engagement groups won't visit due to crime. Some also don't have role models who went to college or vote, and therefore don't see the importance of voting and how the political process benefits them.

Many voter engagement groups have recognized the importance of getting non-college youth politically engaged and are actively developing strategies to do this. Per Rizga (2008),

> When it comes to mobilizing non-college youths, Khari Mosley, the national political director of the League of Young Voters, another

group that works primarily with low-income youth and youth of color, stresses that it's crucial to combine traditional voter organizing tactics, such as canvassing, with new models to engage non-college youth in November. The League plans to use targeted, localized guerrilla marketing tactics, such as Street Teams who post fliers and stickers in clubs, coffee shops and community based organizations. They will also use a balanced mixture of new mediums--including MySpace, Facebook, YouTube, and text messaging--in order to reach the widest number of youths from varying backgrounds. While most youth groups use Facebook as their online organizing destination, the immigrant marches in 2006 revealed that Latino youth still prefer MySpace and text messaging. Most of Black Youth Vote members also use MySpace. Both the League and Voto Latino, the largest online Latino youth voter registration organization, have also learned that using local celebrities such as musicians, actors, and community leaders, rather than famous national stars, brings higher returns when it comes to actually getting young voters to register. In 2006, Voto Latino partnered up with a national Reggaeton celebrity Pitbull. He was able to attract Latino youth to his concerts but it didn't necessarily translate into voter registrations.

After developing a presence in these communities, it is critical that a lasting presence is established. Otherwise, youth will get cynical and not continue their support.

Table 6.1: Votes Cast in Presidential Elections: 1992 - 2004

Source: U.S. Census Bureau, CPS November Voting and Registration
Supplements

Year	Some college			No college		
	18-24	18-29	30 and older	18-24	18-29	30 and older
1972	69.6%	72.5%	85.3%	37.1%	41.8%	64.7%
1976	60.5%	64.2%	81.4%	31.3%	35.0%	61.4%
1980	59.3%	63.7%	84.3%	31.4%	35.3%	64.1%
1984	59.5%	64.1%	83.2%	32.0%	36.3%	64.4%
1988	53.1%	57.8%	80.7%	26.8%	30.3%	60.3%
1992	63.6%	67.2%	84.2%	33.9%	36.4%	62.7%
1996	47.4%	52.0%	74.6%	24.7%	26.0%	53.2%
2000	47.7%	51.8%	74.8%	24.7%	26.7%	53.7%
2004	59.0%	61.1%	77.5%	33.7%	33.7%	56.1%
2008		62.1%			35.9%	

Bibliography

Blades, Meteor. "Youth Voter Turnout Up, But Fails to Break '72 Record." *Daily Kos* (November 5, 2008), http://www.dailykos.com/storyonly/2008/11/5/171841/ 524/28/ 654938

CNN. "Longtime GOP Sen. Arlen Specter becomes Democrat", *CNNPolitics.com* (April 28, 2009), http://www.cnn.com/2009/POLITICS/04/28/specter.party.switch/

Fitzgerald, Mary. *Easier Voting Methods Boost Youth Turnout.* Medford, Massachusetts: The Center for Information and Research on Civic Learning and Engagement, February 2003.

Franceschi, Jela De. "Democrats Mobilize America's Youth Vote." *Voice of America* (April 4, 2008), http://www.voanews.com/english/archive/2008-04/2008-04-10-voa34.cfm

Frum, David. "Why the GOP lost the youth vote." *USA Today* (April 9, 2008), http://blogs.usatoday.com/oped/2008/04/why-the-gop-l-1.html

Graduate School of Political Management. *Young Voter Mobilization Tactics.* Washington, D.C.: The George Washington University, 2006.

Green, Donald P. and Gerber, Alan S. *Get Out the Vote! How to Increase Voter Turnout.* Washington, DC: Brookings Institution Press, 2004.

Hargreaves, Steve. "Exxon posts record $11.68 billion profit." *CNNMoney* (July 31, 2008), http://money.cnn.com/2008/07/31/news/companies/exxon_profits/?post vers ion=2008073110

Howe, Neil and Strauss, William. *Generations: The History of America's Future, 1854-2069.* New York: William Morrow and Co. Inc., 1991.

Howe, Neil and Strauss, William. *Millennials Rising: The Next Generation.* New York: Vintage Books, 2000.

Johnson, Paul. *A History of the American People.* New York: Harper Collins, 1997.

Kirby, Emily Hoban, Samantha Linkins, and Conner Glennon. "State Voter Registration and Election Day Laws". Medford, Massachusetts: The Center for Information and Research on Civic Learning and Engagement, October 2008, http://www.civicyouth.org/PopUps/FS_08_State_Laws.pdf

Kirby, Emily Hoban and Kawashima-Ginsberg, Kei. "The Youth Vote in 2008." Medford, Massachusetts: The Center for Information and Research on Civic Learning and Engagement, April 2009, http://www.civicyouth.org/ PopUps/FactSheets/FS_youth_Voting_2008.pdf

Lancaster, Lynn C. and Stillman, David. *When Generations Collide: Who They Are. Why They Clash. How to Solve the Generational Puzzle at Work.* New York: HarperCollins, 2002.

Lugaila, Terry A. *A Child's Day: 2000 (Selected Indicators of Child Well-Being)*. Washington, D.C.: U.S. Census Bureau, August 2003.

Lopez, Mark Hugo, Emily Kirby, and Jared Sagoff. *The Youth Vote 2004*. Medford, Massachusetts: The Center for Information and Research on Civic Learning and Engagement, July 2005.

Marcelo, Karlo Barrios and Kirby, Emily Hoban. *Quick Facts about U.S. Young Voters: The Presidential Election Year 2008*. Medford, Massachusetts: The Center for Information and Research on Civic Learning and Engagement, 2008.

Marcelo, Karlo Barrios, Margo H. Lopez, Chris Kennedy, and Kathleen Barr. *Young Voter Registration and Turnout Trends*. Medford, Massachusetts: The Center for Information and Research on Civic Learning and Engagement, February 2008.

Musante, Kenneth. "College costs rise." *CNNMoney* (October 29, 2008), http://money.cnn.com/2008/10/29/pf/college/college/index.htm

New Strategist, ed. *The Millennials: Americans Born 1977 to 1994, 3rd edition*. Ithaca, New York: New Strategist Publications, Inc., 2006.

Oshyn, Kristen, and Wang, Tova Andrea. "Youth Vote 2008." *The Century Foundation Issue Brief*, 2008 http://www.tcf.org/publications/electionreform/youthvote.pdf

Reynol, Junco, and Mastrodicasa, Jeanna. *Connecting to the Net.Generation: What Higher Education Professionals Need to Know About Today's Students*. Washington, D.C., NASPA, 2007.

Rizga, Kritina. "Getting Out the (Rest of the) Youth Vote." *Wiretap* (June 23, 2008), http://www.wiretapmag.org/stories/43605/

Rock the Vote! "Young Voter Turnout 2008 – Primaries and Caucuses." (June 4, 2008), http://www.rockthevote.com/assets/publications/electronic-press-kit/young-voter-turnout-in-the.pdf

Roscow, David. *Over Three Million Citizens Under the Age of Thirty Participate in Super Tuesday Primaries: Young Voters Support Obama and Huckabee and McCain*. Medford, Massachusetts: The Center for Information and Research on Civic Learning and Engagement, February 6, 2008.

Starks, Glenn L. "The Effect of Person-Job Fit on the Retention of Top College Graduates in Federal Agencies." *Review of Public Personnel Administration* 27 (2007): 59-70.

Starks, Glenn L. and Brooks, F. Erik. *How Your Government Works: A Topical Encyclopedia of the Federal Government*. Westport, Connecticut: Greenwood Press, 2008.

Tapscott, Don. *Growing Up Digital: The Rise of the Net Generation*. New York: McGraw-Hill, 1998.

U.S. Census Bureau. *Resident Population: National Population Estimates for the 2000s* (2009), http://www.census.gov/popest/national/asrh/2007-nat-res.html

Von Drehle, David. "The Year of the Youth Vote." *Time* (Jan 31, 2008), http://www.time.com/time/politics/article/0,8599,1708570,00.html

Von Drehle, David. "Person of the Year 2008: Why History Can't Wait." *Time* (December 17, 2008), http://www.time.com/time/specials/2008/personof theyear/article/0,31682,1861543_1865068,00.html

About the Author

Dr. Glenn L. Starks holds a Ph.D. in Public Policy and Administration from the Virginia Commonwealth University in Richmond, Virginia. He has approximately twenty years of federal service, and has published books and articles on leadership, disaster relief, affirmative action, supply chain management, and strategic planning in the public organizations.